Mr. and Mrs. C. McDonald Droom

Providence Baptist Church

February 9, 1969.

Dr. Eddings, Teacher

THE GOSPEL IN ISAIAH

The Gospel in Isaiah

By
GILBERT L. GUFFIN

Convention Press
NASHVILLE   TENNESSEE

About the Author

GILBERT L. GUFFIN is a native of Marietta, Georgia and a graduate of Mercer University. He holds the Th.D. degree from Eastern Baptist Seminary and honorary degrees from Mercer University and the Atlanta Law School. He is presently Dean of Religion and Chairman of the Extension Division of Samford University.

Dr. Guffin is author of several books, writer of Sunday School lessons and other materials for various religious periodicals, and has prepared the monthly Bible studies in *Royal Service* on the biblical message of missions.

Originator and first director of the Extension Division of Samford University (formerly Howard College), Dr. Guffin developed a plan since copied by many other colleges. The plan also served as a basis for the development of the Southern Baptist Seminary Extension Program.

The author was president of Eastern Baptist Seminary from 1950 through 1961. During his administration, Eastern Baptist College was founded, and he served it also as president.

Pastor and public school principal for several years in Georgia, Dr. Guffin later served First Baptist Church, Merchantville, New Jersey and First Baptist Church, Jasper, Alabama, as pastor before his first period with Samford. He returned to Samford in 1961. He is married to the former Lorene Parrish, who, before marriage, was the first woman treasurer of Mercer University. They have two sons.

THE GOSPEL IN ISAIAH
and the Crusade of the Americas

C. E. Autrey

THE GOSPEL IN ISAIAH sets forth in reality what Isaiah was saying and makes it applicable to today. Therefore, I think it is a good book to be used in preparation for the Crusade of the Americas.

The book sets forth a fair and honest appraisal of the man Isaiah himself and how he was used of God to speak to the people, warning them and proclaiming to them the good news of God.

In this book, Isaiah is portrayed as one who did not consult with the "powers that be" before he spoke, but he knew God and knew the truth. He spoke the truth in his day. Isaiah was not reluctant to cry out in condemnation of vain, meaningless religious rites; but he was just as quick to set forth the true solemnity of worship. Dr. Guffin points out that worship, as portrayed by Isaiah, is a genuine, solemn business, though it is a source of joy to the one who worships.

I am particularly pleased with the book because it calls attention to the use of evangelism in the day of Isaiah and the use of evangelism today.

Isaiah's concept of the cost of offensiveness against God as set forth in the first chapter is priceless and needs to be given thorough consideration today.

I am happy that Dr. Guffin has clearly called attention to the fact that the hope of redemption was assured to a repentant remnant. The concepts of repentance and redemption are basic and vital in the prophecy of Isaiah and they are basic and vital in the Gospels. It is not difficult to find the good news of the grace of God in Isaiah.

Contents

Church Study Course

THE CHURCH STUDY COURSE began October 1, 1959. It is a merger of three courses previously promoted by the Sunday School Board: the Sunday School Training Course, the Graded Training Union Study Course, and the Church Music Training Course. On October 1, 1961, the Woman's Missionary Union principles and methods studies were added. On January 1, 1967, the Brotherhood Commission principles and methods studies were added.

The course is fully graded. The system of awards provides a series of five diplomas of twenty books each for Adults or Young People, two diplomas of five books each for Intermediates, and two diplomas of five books each for Juniors.

The course is comprehensive, with books grouped into twenty-one categories. The purpose of the course is to help Christians to grow in knowledge and conviction, to help them to grow toward maturity in Christian character and competence for service, to encourage them to participate worthily as workers in their churches, and to develop leaders for all phases of church life and work.

The Church Study Course is promoted by the Baptist Sunday School Board, 127 Ninth Avenue, North, Nashville, Tennessee 37203, through its Sunday School, Training Union, Church Music, and Church Administration departments; by the Woman's Missionary Union, 600 North Twentieth Street, Birmingham, Alabama 35203; by the Brotherhood Commission, 1548 Poplar Avenue, Memphis, Tennessee 38104; and by the respective departments in the states affiliated with the Southern Baptist Convention. A description of the course and the system of awards may be found in the leaflet "Trained Workmen," which may be obtained without charge from any one of these departments.

A record of all awards earned should be maintained in each church. A person should be designated by the church to keep the files. Forms for such records may be ordered from any Baptist Book Store.

Requirements for Credit for Class or Home Study

IF CREDIT IS DESIRED for the study of this book in class or by the home study method, the following requirements must be met:

I. CLASS METHOD

1. The class must meet a minimum of six clock hours. The required time does not include assembly periods.
2. A class member who attends all class sessions and reads the book will not be required to do any written work.
3. A class member who is absent from one or more class sessions must read the book and answer the questions on all chapters he misses.
4. The teacher should request an award for himself. A person who teaches a book in sections for Intermediates or Juniors of any category or conducts an approved unit of instruction for Nursery, Beginner, or Primary children will be granted an award in category 11, Special Studies, which will count as an elective on his own diploma. He should specify in his request the name of the book taught or unit conducted for Nursery, Beginner, or Primary children.

    Credit will be given to "team teachers" when they cooperatively plan the teaching procedures and attend and share responsibility in each teaching session.
5. The teacher should complete the "Request for Book Award" (Form 151) and forward it to the Church Study Course Awards Office, 127 Ninth Avenue, North, Nashville, Tennessee 37203.

II. INDIVIDUAL HOME STUDY

1. A person who does not attend any class session may receive credit by answering all questions for written work as indicated in the book or in a designated periodical. When a person turns in his paper on home study, he must certify that he has read the book.

2. Students may find profit in studying the text together, but individual papers are required. Carbon copies or duplicates in any form cannot be accepted.

3. Home study work papers may be graded by the pastor or a person designated by him, or they may be sent to the Church Study Course Awards Office for grading. The form entitled "Request for Book Award" (Form 151) must be used in requesting awards. It should be mailed to the Church Study Course Awards Office, 127 Ninth Avenue, North, Nashville, Tennessee 37203.

4. Credit for home study of mission study books not containing questions is earned by writing a synopsis of each chapter.

III. Credit for This Book

This book is number 0233 in category 2, section for Adults and Young People.

THE GOSPEL IN ISAIAH

Enrichment resources
for
The Gospel in Isaiah

Four additional correlated resources have been prepared and are available from your Baptist Book Store to enrich your study of this annual Bible Study book. *Study Guide for the Gospel in Isaiah* contains wide margin text of passages to be studied in this book, along with questions to guide you through individual or class study. Teachers will find suggestions in the back of this book for preparation, promotion, and conduct of this annual study. These suggestions have been correlated with the study guide. *The Gospel in Isaiah,* a filmstrip, is also available, with recording, through Baptist Book Stores. Two Broadman books, *God Reigns!* by Leo Green and *Judgment and Redemption in Isaiah* by Page Kelley are available and will provide excellent resource reading for students of this book. Chapters of these two books have been correlated with chapters of the study course book on page 143 of The Gospel in Isaiah.

1

BACKDROP TO A REMARKABLE PROPHECY

AN appraisal of Isaiah by Richard B. Moulton, made near the end of a lifetime spent in the study of great literary works, seems fully warranted: "It may be safely asserted that nowhere else in the literature of the world have so many colossally great ideas been brought together within the limits of a single work." [1]

Elmer A. Leslie correctly wrote, "The book of Isaiah is generally acknowledged to be the greatest of the prophetic books of the Old Testament." [2] Walter Harrelson believes with justification: "The long prophetic book that bears the name of Isaiah of Jerusalem contains not only some of Israel's best literature; it also presents Israelite faith in its most profound expression." [3] Because of its massive ideas, its literary excellence, its expression of Israelite faith at its best, and its many other qualities the prophecy easily deserves the rank of one of the greatest books ever written.

I. THE TOWERING INFLUENCE OF THE BOOK

1. *Its Influence on Hebrew History*

The book of Isaiah contains statements of some of the most distinctive doctrines of the Hebrew faith and

3

gives new depth of meaning to others. This is particularly true of Israel's mission in the world. Long had the idea of a conquering political messiah been held by the Jews. In contrast, the prophet of the Exile set forth the idea of a Suffering Servant.

2. Its Influence on the New Testament

The prophecy of Isaiah is quoted directly or indirectly over and over in the New Testament. One Greek New Testament lists over 190 such passages. (See Westcott and Hort.) [4] This is impressive evidence as to the impact of the book upon those who wrote the Gospels and Epistles.

3. Its Influence on Evangelism and World Missions

The note of evangelism finds reinforcement in many memorable passages in the book. Who can forget the glorious invitation in 55:6-7: "Seek ye the Lord while he may be found, call ye upon him while he is near: Let the wicked forsake his way, and the unrighteous man his thoughts: and let him return unto the Lord, and he will have mercy upon him; and to our God, for he will abundantly pardon"? What evangelist has not felt moved to extend the entreaty found in the same chapter: "Ho, every one that thirsteth, come ye to the waters, and he that hath no money; come ye, buy, and eat; yea, come, buy wine and milk without money and without price" (55:1)?

The era of Amos and Isaiah marks the time of a renewal of the missionary vision imparted earlier to Abraham (Gen. 12:3). While Amos, and perhaps Jonah, deserve to be remembered as early missionaries, Isaiah and Micah were immortal missionary seers. The book of Isaiah, more than any other in the Old Testament, gives emphasis to the truth that through Israel God's glory would be revealed to all nations and "all flesh shall see it together" (40:5). Furthermore, the book's revelation concerning the Suffering Servant whose sacrifice would bring healing to all "literally held the whole world in view and saw it as the object of God's great redemptive compassion and purpose." [5]

So interwoven with the great doctrinal tenets of the Christian faith and mission are the teachings of Isaiah that to disassociate the two would seem a major disaster.

II. THE PROPHET ISAIAH

1. *The Limited Data About Him*

Surprisingly few details are recorded about the personal life of the prophet Isaiah. His father's name was Amoz. It is certain he was not Amos the prophet. Tradition suggests that Isaiah's father was a brother of King Amaziah of Judah. If true, this would have made Isaiah a cousin of King Uzziah. Isaiah would also have been a cousin of Uzziah's successors—Jotham, Ahaz, and Hezekiah.

The prophet Isaiah is thought to have been born around 762–760 B.C. and to have begun his ministry around 742–740 B.C., the final year of Uzziah's reign. The prophecy itself informs us that it was in the year Uzziah died that Isaiah was called to be God's spokesman (6:1–9).

The opening verse of the book tells of the long duration of Isaiah's ministry—through the reigns of Jotham, Ahaz, and Hezekiah of Judah. There is a strong tradition that Isaiah probably lived on into the early reign of the wicked king Manasseh, to as late as 687 B.C., and that he was put to a horrible death by this king for opposition to the latter's idolatry. Some suppose the reference in Hebrews 11:37 to some who were "sawn asunder" may have pertained to Isaiah. If Isaiah was about twenty years old at the time of his call, he apparently lived to be seventy or eighty. He was already married by about 734 B.C. and had two sons, Shear-jashub (7:3) and Maher-shalal-hash-baz (8:3). The names given these sons had prophetic significance. This was especially true of the latter son (8:4). Isaiah's wife was called a "prophetess." This title may have been given her only because she was the wife of the prophet. We have no record of her ever exercising the office herself.

So far as we know, Isaiah spent his entire life in and around Jerusalem. From 2 Chronicles 26:22 and 32:32, we learn that he may have written at least two books besides the one which bears his name, a *Life of King Uzziah*, whom he seems greatly to have loved and admired, and another about Hezekiah and the kings of Judah and Israel.

2. *The Vastness of the Man*

Only a few historical details, such as Isaiah's encouragement of Hezekiah to trust God in days of fearful crisis from siege and famine, are set forth in the prophecy (37:21–35). Yet how much more we know about him! Isaiah's authorship of the entire book which bears his name has come under question from time to time. However, enough is known from what is unquestionably accepted as Isaiah's writing to make us certain that he was one of the most towering and versatile figures of the age.

(1) *A historian.*—Isaiah was obviously an author of note and competence. A literary name does not endure for twenty-seven centuries without a reason. He was regarded also as a historian. The writer, or writers, of 2 Chronicles apparently felt the need of no better authority for the facts recorded in that book than an appeal to the writings of Isaiah.

(2) *Statesman.*—There is considerable evidence to indicate that Isaiah was a statesman of great stature. Consider especially Isaiah's relations with Ahaz and Hezekiah (7:1–25; 20:1–4; 36:1 to 38:22), as well as his amazing understanding of the international situation of his day. Isaiah was a consultant to kings and a man of wisdom and understanding regarding the conditions and future prospects of various nations of his day. He was a person of remarkable farsightedness and one of the most influential men in Judah. The Hebrew scholar Samuel Sandmel wrote: "Isaiah counseled kings and was ignored by them." [6] He was sometimes *heard*, too, and heeded by kings, much to their own and the nation's good.

(3) *Poet.*—Isaiah was not only an author of ability, a historian of note, and a statesman of competence; he was also a poet of rare gift. In truth, most of what we have preserved from his pen was written in poetic form, as can be seen from versions such as the Revised Standard Version or Moffatt's. The use of poetic form discloses the power and beauty, the graphic and picturesque ability of the author. An understanding of his use of poetic imagery to express the revelation given him, therefore, should assist in interpreting Isaiah.

(4) *Servant of God.*—Most of all, Isaiah was God's servant. As such, he became a mighty and fearless preacher, a prophet of peerless power, and a religious leader of enduring influence. Though Isaiah has been described as prince, patriot, and prophet, he was obviously much more. No full explanation of the man and his message is conceivable apart from recognition that the Almighty laid his hand upon him in a special way and used him.

As a writer, and probably as a speaker also, Isaiah was like a master at the console of a great organ. His range seemed to touch every mood and express every level of human emotion. From "trumpet peals of faith, ringing challenge [and] inexorable demands" he could move with unusual effectiveness to "white-hot purity, scorn of all base things, championing of the poor, and tender assurances." [7] It should be noted, also, that Isaiah was able to make use of every style and variety of exposition to communicate the message God had given him.

"The grandeur of his conceptions, his uncompromising emphasis on ethical principles, the vigor of his style, and his command of invective, sarcasm, and irony mark him as one of the most powerful and gifted Hebrew prophets." [8]

3. *His Call and Commitment*

Isaiah felt deeply the demand of his divine call which came in one of the high encounters of God with man (6: 1–8). It was an hour of deep sadness and national mourning, for it was "in the year that king Uzziah died." Some think Isaiah's heaviness of heart was not only because Uzziah, a relative and a great ruler, had been taken, but because of the way he died. It is supposed that Uzziah died the terrible death of a leper. For any heart open to God, the hour of deepest darkness may be the moment when the glory of God is most brilliantly seen. It was so with Isaiah (6:1).

The glory in which God was revealed to Isaiah at once overwhelmed him with a sense of his own sinfulness and of the guilt of his people (6:5). But to those who thus "see" the Lord and sense the depth of their own uncleanness, the voice of the Lord also usually is heard calling them to action. It was so with Isaiah. He heard God asking, "Whom shall I send, and who will go for us?" Having glimpsed the holiness of God and sensing his need and the need of the nation, he could give but one answer: "Here am I; send me." Isaiah knew God's call was for him; he heeded it with total commitment. By any reasonable measurement, he became a spiritual giant.

III. THE WORLD IN WHICH ISAIAH SERVED

In our day of revolution and rebellion, we are given to think that convulsive international conditions are a modern phenomenon. On the contrary, at almost any point in Old Testament times, one will find that similar things were taking place. This was surely true of Isaiah's day. The first twenty years of the prophet's life may have seemed relatively quiet. Uzziah had stabilized his kingdom by this time. But change was taking place elsewhere and was soon to be felt in Judah.

1. His Own Nation

Jotham, son of Uzziah, appears to have taken over the reign of the kingdom, serving in a regency during his father's illness. Possibly Isaiah, who may have been near the age of Jotham, had some uneasiness as to how strong the rule of Jotham would be.

(1) *The reign of Jotham.*—Jotham appears to have followed largely in the footsteps of his father. This may have been due in part to Isaiah's influence upon him. Yet Jotham suffered a losing battle in preventing a rising trend toward idolatry in the land. Rapid spiritual deterioration seriously set in by the latter part of his reign. To Isaiah, this trend could only have been of deepest concern.

(2) *The evil influence of Ahaz.*—Jotham died around 736–735 B.C. and Ahaz, a very evil son, succeeded him. Against Isaiah's advice, Ahaz made an alliance with Tiglath-pileser III, king of increasingly powerful Assyria. Amos had earlier recognized Assyria as a threat to Israel. But Ahaz was in trouble and he needed help. Pekah, king of Israel, and Rezin, king of Syria, were threatening to overthrow Ahaz. In the face of this threat, he turned to Pul (king of Assyria, also called Tiglath-pileser) who was only too glad to get involved in Judah's affairs. However, Isaiah foresaw alliance with Tiglath-pileser as an even more dangerous threat. This was a foresight which time was to verify.

More dangerous and perhaps more agonizing to Isaiah than the alliance was Ahaz' reversal of all the efforts of his father and grandfather to keep the nation true to God. Ahaz closed the Temple to worship of God, first by stripping the Temple itself of all that was of value. He did this to purchase favor with Assyria. Then, under his reintroduction of Baal worship, the Temple doors were finally closed. While these conditions deeply grieved Isaiah, his sorrow was deeper still when Ahaz offered up some of his own sons as sacrifices on heathen altars.

2. *The International Scene as Related to Judah*

(1) *Judah's position in a world of struggle.*—Prosperity and peace had favored the long reign of Uzziah in Judah, just as had been the case with the Northern Kingdom during the reign of Jeroboam II. Great empires were forming in surrounding areas and were constantly struggling for mastery. Rivals for the domination, if not the overthrow, of both Israel and Judah were Phoenicia (Tyre in Amos), Philistia (Gaza in Amos), Edom, and, more importantly, Syria, Assyria, and Egypt. In the beginning of Isaiah's ministry, Assyria was in ascendancy; Babylon, or Chaldea, was later to become dominant. Palestine stood between these nations and served somewhat as a land bridge for trade and commerce. The country was thus caught in most of the intrigues, conflicts, and struggles of their neighbors.

The prophets warned that Israel's strength lay not in alliances with other nations, but in fidelity to the Lord. Assyria (the Nineveh of Jonah's day) brought about the fall of Israel around 722 B.C., in about the twentieth year of Isaiah's ministry in Judah. How much this disaster and its causes, as Isaiah saw them, affected his ministry in Jerusalem thereafter can only be imagined. Surely Isaiah's fear of God's judgment on Judah must have been intensified by Ahaz' wickedness and idol worship. For he was leading Judah over the same road which had led to Israel's ruin. This would help to explain Isaiah's warning to Ahaz against alliances with Pekah and Rezin which were mentioned earlier.

(2) *A good king intervenes.*—Surprisingly, Hezekiah proved to be a good son of a bad father. The reason seems largely that he had respect for Isaiah and listened to his counsel. As already noted, it was Isaiah's advice and encouragement which led Hezekiah to resist all threats from siege and famine imposed by Sennacherib of Assyria. Isaiah persuaded the king not to allow the national leaders to pressure him into alliance with Egypt. Surrender to Sennacherib or an alliance with Egypt would have been disastrous. (See 2 Kings 18:20-21.)

(3) *Darkening days versus enduring hope.*—Manasseh was everything his father Hezekiah was not. Raised to the throne when he was only twelve years of age (2 Kings 21:1), his reign of fifty-five years led Judah steadily downward, both spiritually and morally. Indifferent to, if not contemptuous of the aging Isaiah, his father's trusted adviser, Manasseh reestablished Baal worship and erected altars to idols even in the Temple itself. He is said also to have "made his son pass through the fire" (2 Kings 21:6). This means that he likely offered him as a sacrifice to heathen gods, a practice followed by his grandfather Ahaz. This was only one of Manasseh's sins against God and Israel.

The prophet seemed to see beyond Ahaz' and even Manasseh's failures and wickedness to a glorious day when God would fulfil his ancient covenant.

Whether one believes that all of the book of Isaiah was the work of the prophet Isaiah or that some part was the work of a later writer, clearly the Exile is the major situation understood in Isaiah 40–66. The prophet was speaking of that time when Jerusalem fell to Babylon, and its people were taken captives to a

being God's channel of blessing to all nations (Gen. 12:2–3). Israel seemed determined to forfeit her responsibility and to rebel against God. The realization of this was like a fire in the prophet's bones.

1. God's Complaint Justifiable (1:2–4)

The complaint of God seemed so justifiable, as well as so terrible, that Isaiah was moved to call upon the heavens to listen and the whole earth to give ear to what God had to say (1:2). The God who spoke through Isaiah is not a capricious, ruthless diety; nor is he austere, vengeful, and remote. Instead, he is a loving, merciful Father. Though Isaiah did not use the word "father" in this connection, his inference is clear. He quoted God as saying, "I have nourished and brought up children, and they have rebelled against me" (v. 2). Not only had God delivered this nation out of its suffering and anguish in Egyptian bondage; he had adopted them as his own children. Indeed, the Hebrew here is literally: "Sons I have reared [or begotten] and brought up." These words give special emphasis to God's fatherly care. Though Israel was related to God by adoption, they were declared to be his own children. The thought is rich both in its actual meaning and in what it movingly connotes.

More is indicated here than the mere "fatherhood of God," as that phrase is now understood. Israel had become his sons through God's love and grace and by his own choice and redemptive work. God had been faithful to the uttermost. In the time of their helplessness in Egypt and in their long wandering in the wilderness, he had been with them. He had brought them to maturity as a nation in the land promised them. He had given such evidence of his love and care that no eye could fail to behold it. No wonder the prophet was moved to call upon the hosts of heaven and all the peoples of the earth to behold the scandal of the indifference, ingratitude, and inconceivable rebellion of children who, though so favored, had turned away from their Father!

The greatest evil of the people was not merely that they had not responded to the love shown them and the care given them as they ought. It was that they had actually turned in the opposite direction. "And they have rebelled against me," God charged. After all, that is basically what sin is—rebellion against the God who in love and mercy is not only Creator but Father. To flout and turn against a law which fellowmen have formulated is one thing; it is quite another thing to flout and turn against the known desires of a Father who compassionately loves and faithfully cares for his children. The latter response must be labeled "rebellion."

At this point Isaiah inferred a truth about the nature of God that is both inspiring and reassuring: The Almighty God is a Heavenly Father; he is a personal God. Hence, man can come into vital personal relationship with him.

Isaiah's stirring reminder of God's love and care ought to have melted the coldest heart in Israel. Yet, he had to add: "The ox knoweth his owner, and the ass his master's crib: but Israel doth not know, my people doth not consider" (v. 3). This pastoral scene, familiar to everyone who heard the prophet's voice, pointed up a persistent paradox: How could a people, so enlightened and favored of God as was Israel, become so indifferent to him as this comparison suggests? Plaintive and full of pathos, the picture painted here should remind us of the scene when Christ wept over Jerusalem, saying, "How often would I . . . and ye would not!" (Luke 13:34). Even the ox recognizes the one to whom he belongs, and the ass remembers the source of his nourishment, but a people helpless and hopeless apart from God's mercy "doth not know, . . . doth not consider."

Three verbs are used in Isaiah 1:4 to describe the consequences: "forsaken," "provoked," "gone away backward." The opening expression in the verse carries the force of "shame on." What shame ought to be heaped upon this kind of disloyalty and unwillingness to respond in loving obedience to the God who is the source of all good things.

The phrase "they are gone away backward" is better translated, "they are utterly estranged" (RSV). Their rebellion against their Heavenly Father made them an alien nation.

The whole prophecy is filled with such divine complaints as the one in 1:1–2. And one has only to read the history of God's chosen people to see how justifiable were those complaints.

2. *The Nation's Guilt Inexcusable* (29:13–17)

All men are held morally responsible for their decisions and deeds. This is perhaps the reason prophecies affecting the judgment of other nations besides Judah are found also in Isaiah.

Much that appears in chapters 1–5 of the book is thought to have been uttered during the days of Ahaz. It likely followed Ahaz' refusal to give heed to the warnings of the prophet and, thus, it affected Judah primarily. The chief emphasis of this section is that the guilt of the people to whom the message was first delivered was inexcusable. This fact will be reemphasized often in the book. A further example is found in a setting which apparently concerned Judah's intrigues with Egypt. Once again the inexcusable nature of the nation's guilt is impressively declared (29:13–17). This particular passage reveals that a form of worship still did exist. The tragedy was not that the practices of worship were neglected but that "worship" was only from the mouth. "This people draw near me with their mouth," it is sadly observed, "and with their lips do honour me."

What good is it to draw near to God only with one's mouth? The singing of the most inspired music, even the psalms of David, would be but a mockery unless the music sprang out of devotion to the Lord. Wisdom and discernment perish among those who fail to see this truth (v. 14).

What success can anyone expect who tries to hide his evil heart and purpose from the Lord? Only those who deceive themselves will believe God does not observe (v. 15).

The Revised Standard Version helps us here to see how pointed this verse really is: "Woe to those who hide deep from the Lord their counsel, whose deeds are in the dark, and who say, 'Who sees us? Who knows us?'" (29:15). The verse may refer to the many sins of which the people were guilty. Or, it may refer to the intrigues they were attempting in their efforts to make alliances with Egypt for revolt against Assyria instead of seeking the Lord as the source of their strength. Whatever the prophet had in mind, God could only pronounce, as he often did through Isaiah, a "woe" to those who deceive themselves. Their guilt was the more inexcusable because it was a guilt of self-deception. Truly it could be said of these, "You turn things upside down!" (v. 16, RSV). Or, as another translation has it: "Things are upside down because of you."

What a vivid way to describe man's sin of self-deception! For a man to assume he can exclude God from his world and walk in his own way without regard to Divine guidance or will is as audacious as for the clay in the pottery to assume it is as great as the potter, or for a thing created to deny its own maker.

Isaiah may not have been as colorful and caustic as Amos in describing the sins of his people, but he was no less specific.

II. THE WARNINGS AND PLEAS OF GOD PROCLAIMED (1:10–20,24–31; 65:1–3)

A denomination or a nation is in trouble when its people give lip service to God, when activities of the churches become perfunctory, when worship services are meaningless religious rites and empty formalities. Tendencies in this direction which exist in our nation today properly give cause for alarm. It was about similar conditions that Isaiah was alarmed and out of which he was moved most forcefully to speak.

1. Condemnation of Vain, Meaningless Religious Rites (Activities) (1:10–18)

The voice of Isaiah thundered against the carrying out of mere religious forms. However extensive and prolific these were, they failed to express true devotion to God. "To what purpose," he understands God as asking, "is the multitude of your sacrifices unto me?" The degree of prosperity then prevalent in Judah enabled the people to bring many lambs and other well-fed beasts to the Temple. But God replied to these meaningless religious performances, "I delight not in the blood of bullocks, or of lambs, or of he goats" (1:11).

(1) *True solemnity of worship unacknowledged* (1:11–12,14).—God had ordered that no more vain offerings be brought before him. These were offerings which were empty of meaning, which had no sense of true worship in them. They were rites not prompted by devotion, a real desire for forgiveness, or a genuine intention of turning away from evil. There was no moral obedience to accompany the sacrifices.

The observing of special occasions such as new moons and sabbaths and the calling of assemblies, under such circumstances, were only an abomination to God. To him who saw deeper than the surface, such gatherings only profaned his presence and name. No wonder God said, "They have become a burden to me, I am weary of bearing them" (1:14, RSV).

(2) *No conscience as to the worshiper's own iniquity* (1:15–18).—The genuine worship of God, though marked with joy and inexpressible delight, is also solemn business. Incessant examination of one's motive is essential. Those who do not thus guard themselves may fall prey to the tragic plight of those people whom Isaiah warned: "And when ye spread forth your

hands, I will hide mine eyes from you: yea, when ye make many prayers, I will not hear" (1:15).

Their hands were full of blood. The reason was that, in God's sight, their hearts were filled with lust, greed, injustice, and indifference both to God and to those for whom they were responsible. Man's reason has failed him when he assumes that regardless of the manner of his life he can still lift up prayers to God in the same casual way. The only appropriate prayer from one besmirched by sin is the plea for God's mercy. God proclaims: "Wash you, make you clean; put away the evil of your doings from before mine eyes; cease to do evil; Learn to do well; seek judgment, relieve the oppressed, judge the fatherless, plead for the widow." God is not only offended by man's sins but also by the shallow view men hold concerning their sin. The prophet was warning that God simply will not hear the petitions of such persons. "I will not listen; your hands are full of blood" (1:15, RSV).

The traditional view of verse 18 has seen in these words a gracious invitation to partake of God's mercy. Many have heard and responded to such an appeal and have found forgiveness for their sins. Some scholars hold an entirely different interpretation. It, too, is instructive to those who need to see that God will not look with favor on the petition of one who has continued to sin against him. These scholars see this verse phrased as a question: "Come, now, let us present our cases as though we were in a court of law [such is the meaning of 'reason together']: If your evil deeds are like scarlet, are they going to be judicially deemed to be white as snow? If they are red as crimson, can they be white as wool?"[1] Regardless of which interpretation is the more acceptable (or accurate), it is clear that the prophet wanted hearers and readers to be reminded of the righteousness of God and of his displeasure with evil.

2. The Cost of Offenses Against God (1:20–31)

In awesome terms Isaiah continued his warning to a disobedient and wilful people: "But if ye refuse and rebel, ye shall be devoured with the sword: for the mouth of the Lord hath spoken it" (v. 20).

The verses which follow (21–23) describe the nature of some of the offenses of which the people were guilty. They are a lament over Jerusalem's moral condition. The warning, then, is again resumed as to what sin, unrepented of, will cost: "And I will turn my hand upon thee, and purely [thoroughly] purge away thy dross, and take away all thy tin." Something like the refiner's fire of which Malachi spoke (Mal. 3:2–3) must have been in the prophet's mind here. Through the purging process predicted, destruction will come to the transgressors (literally, rebels). Those who forsake the Lord will be consumed by judgment as tin or alloy is consumed by the refiner's fire. Only pure gold can endure the test.

One writer has referred to the first nine verses of chapter one as "The Great Arraignment." Perhaps most of the rest of the chapter could as well be entitled "The Great Argument." This argument is based first upon the appeal of reason; second, on the certain consequences of rebellion. These two great themes constitute two of the major concerns which, in general, are found throughout the book. Even in chapter

65, the reminder is given: "I was ready to be sought by those who did not ask for me; I was ready to be found by those who did not seek me. . . . I spread out my hands all the day to a rebellious people, who walk in a way that is not good, following their own devices" (vv. 1–2, RSV). There is frequent interweaving in the book of these great themes as well as repetition of them. They are not the only themes stressed however. A third should also be noted.

III. The Hope of Redemption Assured to a Repentant Remnant (1:9,19; 10:19–22; 46:3–4; 65:8–10)

Blazing with a brilliance possibly surpassing all the rest of the Old Testament is the message of hope which shines forth from the last section of Isaiah. That hope is extended specifically to the exiled people of Judah who would repent and meet the conditions for its realization. To the repentant remnant, glorious assurances were set forth in surpassing tenderness. For these God's unfailing care is guaranteed: "Hearken to me, O house of Jacob, all the remnant of the house of Israel, who have been borne by me from your birth, carried from the womb; even to your old age I am He, and to gray hairs I will carry you. I have made, and I will bear; I will carry and will save" (46:3–4, RSV).

This section (chaps. 40–66) has been referred to as "The Prophecies of Peace," or "The Book of Comfort." It would be difficult, in truth, to find an adequate title to cover the exalted expressions of comfort, peace, and hope especially set forth in this part of Isaiah. Many similar passages are contained also in the first thirty-nine chapters. Indeed, so great is the good news found in *all* these passages that a special study of them seems in order.

IV. THE EMPHASIS OF THIS STUDY

Isaiah is so massive that a comprehensive treatment, at least within the limits of the present purpose, would be virtually impossible. We shall devote ourselves in this study to those passages which relate most nearly to the concept of grace.

Isaiah, like Jeremiah and some other books of both the Old and New Testaments, follows no chronology. At times the historical circumstances surrounding portions of the book are difficult to discern even with the closest examination. In recent times, considerable diversity of opinion as to the dating of these parts of the book has been expressed. This problem has contributed also to differences of opinion as to authorship of the various sections of the book. It is sufficient for our present purpose merely to take brief note of some of the reasons why these differences have risen.

Most scholars agree there is a marked distinction between chapters 1–39 and 40–66. The first thirty-nine chapters emphasize judgment; the last twenty-seven, grace, hope, and peace. Historical material is clearly evident in only a few places, as in chapters 36–39. Elsewhere the date of the writing of the material must be judged largely, or entirely, by other factors.

The traditional theory, held until comparatively recently, is that the entire book which bears his name was written by Isaiah of Jerusalem. Jewish statements dating back to at least the second century B.C. attribute the entire book to Isaiah. The Dead Sea Scrolls, discovered in 1947, reveal that by the second century B.C. the book was recognized as a unity and had no break between chapter 39 and the rest.

The view that Isaiah, son of Amoz, wrote all the book has come under question by many. One reason is that the latter section of the book has reference to the period of the Exile or later. Those who hold the traditional theory that Isaiah wrote all the book believe that which related to the future was especially revealed to the prophet long before the events took place. Isaiah, these hold, foresaw by divine revelation the Babylonian exile and even the deliverance of God's remnant from captivity. Other scholars in recent times have concluded that portions of the book, especially chapters 40–66, were written by another, or by several others.

Some scholars say that it is possible that brief parts of chapters 40–66 may date back to Isaiah's day, but they think the section as a whole did not come from his pen. And two reasons are given for this position. First, such specific details of the distant future as references to Cyrus who lived nearly two centuries (150 years) later could hardly have been known by Isaiah. Furthermore, from the contents of this section (40–66) the Exile seems already to have become a reality. The great chapter on comfort (chap. 40), it is reasoned, could hardly have had meaning in Isaiah's day. However, to a people already in captivity it would have been a most appropriate and welcomed message. Furthermore, it is held that all Old Testament prophets tended to speak primarily to the people of their own times and to give a message immediately relevant to circumstances and needs of that day. On this view some hold that chapters 40–66, which largely look to the future, could hardly have been expected from Isaiah of Jerusalem.

Those holding to this position feel that if the prophecy of Isaiah 40–66 had existed as early as the eighth century B.C., it would be difficult to conceive how men could have believed that Jerusalem and the Temple would not fall. (See Jer. 7.)

Francisco, respected professor of Old Testament, wisely notes, however, that the argument resolves itself largely into "theological hairsplitting." A good part of it depends upon what view one holds regarding inspiration and the supernatural. It is enough to remember that, whatever the date and whoever the author, the message of the prophecy is from God.

Discussions over the authorship of Isaiah should not become a source of real disturbance to anyone. Whatever view we may be persuaded to accept as to its human authorship, our chief concern should be to discover what the book, in God's purpose, now says to us. The fact that the writer of the book is nowhere named in its contents directs attention from human authorship to the Holy Spirit who inspired the writing.

Accepting the book of Isaiah as the authoritative Word of God given, as were the rest of Scriptures, for the spiritual enlightenment and the eternal hope of mankind, our attempt in the remaining chapters will be to see what God says, particularly in the latter part of the book, concerning his great redemptive plan for all the world. The evangelical nature of the material, the doctrinal truth set forth, and the foreshadowing of the coming of Christ it so clearly foretells constitute what we may readily call THE GOSPEL IN ISAIAH. This grand theme is the focus of the following chapters.

[1] G. Ernest Wright, *Isaiah*, Layman's Bible Commentaries (London: SCM Press, 1964), p. 25.

3

GOD'S MESSAGE OF COMFORT
AND ASSURANCE

THE GRANDEUR of the book of Isaiah is nowhere more apparent than in Isaiah 40. At no time before Jesus stood by the brokenhearted sisters at Lazarus' tomb was the tender, comforting concern of God more memorably expressed. The words which open the chapter have been reassuringly repeated at countless funerals and have been the solace of millions.

This chapter introduces a section which concerns a period before the agony of the Exile was ended. To the exiles these words provided comfort and hope that the Exile was near an end and that God would intervene in history to bring salvation. Regardless of one's position on the authorship of the passage, its meaning and message are clear—for the first hearers and for us today. It brings a message of hope and comfort from God to his people.

The chapter contains not merely a call for God's people to be comforted. It is a revelation of the grounds for that comfort.

I. THE HEAVENLY VOICES (40:1-11)

Voices seem to echo back and forth in this passage as in a heavenly chamber. Many scholars see in these

verses a heavenly council and think it was a call to the
prophet who was to deliver God's message. It is clear
that the voices which spoke were from more than one
source. One writer refers to them as "The Four Herald
Voices." [1]

The backdrop, whether foreseen or immediate, is
the painful and trying period of the Exile. The solemnity and suffering of the people at the time are clearly
in view. Discouragement and hopelessness were settling
down upon them. In the darkness of that time of near
despair a voice was heard, and other voices then took
up the theme.

1. *The Comforting Voice* (40:1-2)

"Comfort ye, comfort ye my people, saith your
God." The source of this glorious consolation is identified as "your God." To those who had begun to doubt
that God cared or took note of them anymore, the
assuring words, "your God," are impressively accented. Jesus struck a similar note when he taught us
to pray, "Our Father which art in heaven." Inciden-
tally, the phrase "saith your God" is peculiar to, and
often repeated throughout, the prophecy of Isaiah. The
message is addressed to Jerusalem as representing the
people of God (v. 2). Jerusalem had been the spiritual
center and political capital of Judah. Thus, it repre-
sented the whole nation.

The tender consolation of the thought is better revealed in a literal rendering of the phrase "speak ye
comfortably," which is "speak ye to the heart."

The past iniquity of the people is not denied or ignored. In truth, it is and must be recognized. But regarding Judah, God now proclaimed, "Her iniquity is

pardoned"—or, more exactly, "paid off," "accepted," or "absolved." Her draft, time of military service, or "warfare" spent in exile was at an end. She had suffered long enough; God now assured forgiveness.

The phrase, "received of the Lord's hand double for all her sins," perhaps reflects the idea expressed in the Mosaic law that those who took what was not their own were to make twofold restitution. Here it is apparently used to emphasize that the "warfare," or suffering of the nation, was now completely or doubly fulfilled. The phrase should not be interpreted to mean that God had afflicted them mercilessly or excessively. He had only permitted what their own sins and rebellion had brought upon them. Furthermore, he had had to wait to deliver them until, as we shall later see, their own hearts and attitudes would allow his help.

2. The Commanding Voice (40:3–6a)

This voice is not identified. It is thought to have a celestial source. What is spoken also may have had primary reference to the spiritual renewal of the people. Israel was called upon to respond by faith and to "prepare . . . the way of the Lord." She had suffered much. Now God in his marvelous grace would deliver her. The point here is that the Lord is about to lead his people back from exile. It is a declaration of the Lord's imminent action. The New Testament makes clear that this prophesy ultimately found a voice in John the Baptist.

3. The Concerned Voice (40:6b–8)

Possibly it is the prophet who now responded to the awesome and glorious call issued earlier. He had been ordered to preach (or cry) unto the people. But what could he "cry"? Desolation and dismay had brought deep, sheer pessimism and had left no hope: "All flesh is grass. . . . The grass withereth" (vv. 6–7). This was to say that there was in sight no prospect of the deliverance the prophet was called to proclaim. He saw no reason for hope unless it was in the enduring Word of God. If God proclaimed it, then there was hope. In contrast with the perishable nature of flesh, God's Word is imperishable.

"But the word of our God shall stand for ever" (v. 8) may be interpreted as the divine response to the dismal attitude of prophet and people. At any rate, the verses suggest that the final, the best, and the most precious hope and assurance to which any despairing people may cling is God and his Word. Though heaven and earth pass away, his revealed Word remains the basis of steadfast certainty. His promises are immutable.

4. *The Exultant Voice* (40:9–11)

It is not clear as to whether these verses comprise a further part of the message of the heavenly voice just heard or more of the prophet's own response. Whichever it was, the magnificent, poetic call expressed was designed to awaken the people of God to the thrill and wonder of the joyous news that exile would soon be ended. Soon the awful pain and humiliation of captivity would be over.

The phrase "good tidings" used here is thought to be the first specific reference found in the Old Testament to the "gospel" (good news). The good tidings were tidings of deliverance of Judah from captivity and of her spiritual renewal. Thus, they had both a historical and a spiritual significance. This is the basic meaning of the gospel. The New Testament word denotes the good news of God's salvation through Christ from the captivity of sin.

As 41:25 and especially 45:1 indicate, the immediate deliverance referred to in this whole context was that which would take place under Cyrus, king of Persia. Assyria first brought oppression upon Judah and especially on Israel. Assyria was later destroyed, and Babylon became the dominant world power. Finally, it was Babylon which took Judah into captivity. But the larger and more enduring significance of the passage, from the New Testament viewpoint, is the fulfilment it had in the redemptive work of Christ. He who was Conqueror and Ruler is also the Shepherd of the flock (v. 11). (See also Luke 1:50–55, 68–75; John 10:1–18.)

II. THE INFINITE POWER AND WISDOM OF GOD (40:12–17)

The preceding passage (9–11) is an inspiring appeal to faith in God. Verses 12–17 begin a description of the nature of God, the eloquence of which would be difficult to match. The majestic greatness and universal sovereignty of God are set forth by a series of three penetrating questions. These are followed by three great responses:

> Who has measured the waters in the
>   hollow of his hand
>   and marked off the heavens with a span,
> enclosed the dust of the earth in a measure
>   and weighed the mountains in scales
>   and the hills in a balance?

Who has directed the Spirit of the Lord,
　or as his counselor has instructed him?
Whom did he consult for his enlightenment,
　and who taught him the path of justice,
and taught him knowledge,
　and showed him the way of understanding?

Behold, the nations are like a drop
　　from a bucket,
　and are accounted as the dust on the scales;
behold, he takes up the isles like fine dust.

Lebanon would not suffice for fuel,
　nor are its beasts enough for a burnt offering.

All the nations are as nothing before him,
　they are accounted by him as less
　　than nothing and emptiness.
　　　　　　　　　—Isaiah 40: 12–17, RSV

Could there be a more thought-provoking word picture of the greatness of God? Both philosophy and
logic are challenged to conceive a god more glorious
than the living God. No answer to what is asked in
the text seems possible except the one inferred and the
one to which all creation testifies: God. And he is the
God who has both forgiven the iniquity of his people
and will be as a shepherd to them. He will gather "the
lambs with his arm." Can any man who knows such a
God be afraid of the future or fall into despair over his
present trial? Compared to the Lord God, all nations
are as nothing—even "less than nothing."

III. THE LIVING GOD, NOT HELPLESS IDOLS, MAN'S
　　HOPE (40: 18–26)

How pitiful and tragic it is when men choose for
themselves lesser gods than the living God! But there

were "god" factories then, as there still are. "To whom then will ye liken God?" How the gods to which men still turn shrivel when compared to the Creator and Lord of all the universe!

Idols were common in Babylon. Some Jewish exiles may even have been tempted at times to feel that those who trusted in these gods fared better than they. Was God, after all, what they supposed him to be? Yes, and more—infinitely more! Even "nations are as a drop of [literally, a drop in or from] a bucket." They are relatively insignificant compared to him. In truth, they are as "dust on the scales" (RSV), so insignificant as to make no noticeable difference in the weight on the balances.

Some think there is in this passage an echo of the dialogue the prophet may have had with fellow exiles. Could their complaints have provoked this powerful portrayal of the living God? Only inspired insight could have so comprehended the vastness and glory of the living God.

The gods men make, whether images carved by hand or other objects of worship such as power, money, or even their own persons, can but fail them. Only to mention the vanity of such idolatry seems enough for the prophet. Without specifically stating the helplessness of these gods and the hopelessness of all who trust in them, he turned his glance toward the God "that sitteth upon the circle of the earth" (40:22). This vision is climaxed with a great, abiding assurance; "He is strong in power; not one faileth."

The verb "hath created" in verse 26 is characteristic of the latter part of Isaiah. It is used nearly twenty times there. If God is the creator of man and the universe, cannot he also be the Saviour of man and the ruler of the universe?

Verses 25–27 repeat an earlier thought (v. 18) and take it to new heights. No one can be made "equal" to God. To him who has eyes to see, the whole universe gives witness of God's creative power and wisdom. Of the immeasurable starry host, not one fails in its course. He created and he sustains them all.

IV. THE ENDURING AND EMPOWERING GRACE OF GOD (40:27–31)

Judah greatly needed the assurance that God was able to deliver her and that he truly cared for her. Evidence of this is in the complaint disclosed in 40:27 (RSV):

> Why do you say, O Jacob,
>   and speak, O Israel,
> "My way is hid from the Lord,
>   and my right is disregarded by my God"?

Ours are not the only times characterized by complaint about peoples' rights! In that day, some were brazenly charging not that men but God disregarded certain rights.

The answer came to Israel in an unforgettable assurance. A modern paraphrase of it might be: "Don't you know that God, the Creator of time and space, is not dead? He has not fainted, become silent, or given up. He understands and sympathizes unceasingly. In him are found the needed resources always."

The phrase, "there is no searching of his understanding," does not refer primarily to God's infinite knowledge. It points to the fathomless depths of his understanding of man's need. Israel had feared and possibly complained that their "way" was hidden from, unknown to, or unnoticed by God. The answer to that fear is lastingly given. Not only does the everlasting God never faint or grow weary, but he gives power to the faint and strength to the weak. Seeing this, men are moved to exclaim: "Great is our Lord, and of great power: his understanding is infinite" (Psalm 147:5).

Is it possible that men, if they had known such a God as this, could have assumed that he had disregarded them or could not deliver them?

Surely Israel needed a new discovery of God's grace and enduring power. To people whose faith had been blunted so long by suffering and the sight of idol worship, the majestic words spoken by the prophet must have sounded like heavenly music.

> They who wait for the Lord
> shall renew their strength,
> they shall mount up with wings like eagles,
> they shall run and not be weary,
> they shall walk and not faint.
>
> —Isaiah 40:31, RSV

Israel in exile was "faint" spiritually, not just physically and in morale. For the first time, probably, she really felt the poignancy of her spiritual need. But God would give "power" to the faint, and to those who had "no might" he would give strength. Israel's very sense of helplessness and unworthiness afforded an opportunity such as had not previously existed for God to provide his strength. Many times in the history of Israel, God could not give help because of their self-sufficiency. Jesus' teaching in the Sermon on the Mount suggests that self-sufficiency closes the door to God's special mercy. Only to the "poor in spirit" is it always assured that "theirs is the kingdom of heaven."

The grievous test of the Exile may have been difficult even to the very young. It was so severe that it caused young men to fall exhausted (v. 30). Yet "they that wait upon the Lord shall renew their strength." Such waiting was to be characterized by patient confidence and unfailing trust. To wait on him is to exercise un-qualified faith in and steadfast loyalty and devotion to him. To wait on the Lord in the biblical sense is never a quiescent, stoical, irresponsible passing of time. It requires that one get in step with God's plan and purpose, knowing that his promises do not fail to those who meet his conditions, that for such persons his power and grace are sufficient.

The order of promises given in verse 31 at first seems anticlimactic: to "mount up," to "run," to "walk." It may reflect the sequence of Israel's response as she received knowledge of her coming deliverance from bondage. The initial reaction to the news would bring an excitement best described as soaring on eagle's wings. Then the desire to be free would lead to their running toward its realization. In the long, hard "walk" back to the land of their dreams, hopes, and love, how-ever, they would not faint.

Here was God's glorious and exalted answer to his peoples' spirit of defeat and despair. He whose great-ness is such that the nations are to him as a "drop from a bucket" has his hands on his own. They, therefore, need not faint or fail. "The chapter begins with the assurance being given to the heart of Israel that their God was certain to redeem and restore them; it now draws to its magnificent close, bidding them hope in the Lord, who is so mighty and merciful." [2]

In verses 12–31, the sunrise of the original gospel of the prophet is disclosed. The message is addressed to both Jew and Gentile: to the former to renew their confidence in their God, and to the latter to elicit response to God's claims upon them.

In this great chapter then, we find not only one of the mountain peaks of divine comfort but also apparently the first appearance on history's landscape of both the word for "gospel," as the New Testament knows it, and of the full assurance that gospel affords.

---

[1] George Adam Smith, *The Book of Isaiah* (London: Hodder & Stoughton, 1900), p. 71.

[2] Davidson, Stibbs, and Kevan, *The New Bible Commentary* (Grand Rapids: Eerdmans Publishing Company, 1953), p. 589.

4

GOD'S MARVELOUS GRACE

Though brilliant efforts have been made to define the biblical meaning of grace, no definition quite equals the revelation of God's grace as seen in human experience. For example, John Newton, out of deliverance from a life of sin and degradation, could speak movingly of "amazing grace . . . that saved a wretch like me." Newton felt as deeply the wonder of God's grace as did any man. Yet not even he, with all his remarkable poetic gifts, was able to define or describe it as well as his life demonstrated it. He used to explain that the crowds which attended his services did not come to hear him preach. With the curiosity of people who wish to see lions tamed at a circus, they came to behold him as a trophy of God's grace.

In the passage under study, and to some degree in the entire prophecy of Isaiah, something of the same idea is suggested. The thoughtful reader of Isaiah is constantly aware of God's patience and grace toward his people.

It is striking that in not one instance in the whole book of Isaiah does the word "grace" appear. (The phrase "be gracious unto" is used three times—in Isa. 30:18–19; 33:2.) But few books contain more evidence of the work and nature of God's grace. Certain selections chosen from chapters 41, 42, and 43, as well as the contexts out of which they are taken, afford notable examples of what is meant by God's grace.

I. GOD'S PEOPLE NEED HAVE NO FEAR (41:10-20)

In the opening part of this chapter, especially in verses 1-5, the prophet apparently was speaking of the anticipated rise of Cyrus of Persia as God's instrument through whom deliverance would be brought to Israel. As yet, Cyrus was either unknown or only slightly known. The situation of which the prophet spoke was that which related to an Israel already in exile. Babylon, who brought the Jews into captivity, seemed an unchallengeable power. But foresight was given the prophet to recognize a course of coming events which would change the world of that day and, in changing it, open the door of freedom to the exiles. What he foresaw came to pass, for Cyrus conquered Media in 550 B.C., Lydia in 546 B.C., and Babylon in 539 B.C. God was working in history even as the prophet foretold.

1. The Reason to Be Free of Fear (41:10-19)

God had especially chosen and called Jacob, or Israel (vv. 8-9), for a unique mission in the world. (Though the Northern Kingdom was called Israel, after the fall of that kingdom and especially during the Exile, the people of Judah came to be known by the original name of Israel.) God's original purpose for the nation had not been annulled or forgotten. He had "taken" them "from the ends of the earth." The other nations all about were now trembling before the dangers which beset them, but Israel need not be afraid.

History relates a dramatic, if tragic, story of how rich King Croesus of Lydia sent emissaries about this time to all surrounding nations—even to the gods of Delphi. By presenting magnificent gifts, he sought to learn from the gods what to expect as to the threat posed by Cyrus. In that revolutionary day when nations and empires were falling, God had his eyes upon his Chosen People. Though they were scattered to the ends of the earth, he would recall them for the fulfilment of the mission to which he had originally appointed them.

(1) *The assurances afforded Israel* (41:10–14).— "Fear thou not" is, therefore, the divine assurance God inspired the prophet to proclaim. The verbs used to support this assurance are impressively stacked one upon another:

> "Fear thou not" (v. 10)
> "Be not dismayed" (v. 10)
> "Fear not" (v. 13)
> "Fear not" (v. 14)

Equally noticeable is the accumulation of the phrases in which assurance is given:

> "I am with thee" (v. 10)
> "I am thy God" (v. 10)
> "I will strengthen thee" (v. 10)
> "I will help thee" (v. 10)
> "I will uphold thee" (v. 10)

(2) *The humiliation of Israel* (41:14).—The assurance so abundantly reinforced here is not based upon Israel's merit but upon God's mercy. This is reflected in the remark, "Fear not, thou worm Jacob, and ye men of Israel." The remark also suggests the condition of the people. Debased, poor, and helpless in their captivity, they must have now felt themselves

little better than worms in the dust of Babylon. Some think the words were spoken endearingly as though God was saying, "Fear not, thou worm Jacob, thou little worm Israel." But the remark appears to be a recognition of the weakness and humiliation which had overtaken a once so proud and confident people. At last, the people were in a state which opened the door for God to help them.

We moderns have an aversion toward words such as, "Would he devote that sacred head for such a worm as I?" The substitution of terms more complimentary to ourselves may be an ominous sign. One usually does not have genuine conviction of sin and a compelling sense of his need of salvation who does not also feel an unworthiness and helplessness akin to that which Israel experienced at this crucial time. It is evident that in her humiliation Israel was nearer deliverance and the divine display of mercy than she had been in over a hundred years. "I will help thee, saith the Lord, and thy redeemer, the Holy One of Israel."

(3) *The supernatural work of the Lord* (41:15, 18).—From its humbled position, likened unto a worm in the dust, Israel was to be transformed into a "potent force" of judgment upon other nations about them. Note, for example, the fruitless attempts of other nations later to stop the work of rebuilding the walls of Jerusalem under Nehemiah (Neh. 6:1–16).

God planned more for Israel than a recognition of unworthiness and sinfulness. The people must become stalwart in God's strength. They must be changed from "worms" to "threshing sledges." Not only were they destined to encounter human foes, but the appalling toughness of the route back home was before them.

Those who have personally traversed the arid, mountainous, and forbidding regions which lay between Babylon and Jerusalem can appreciate more deeply the seriousness of the test Israel was now to face. It was almost enough in itself to make the people, though on the very threshold of deliverance, give up and settle back down in their captive role. It seems that many decided to do just this. Apparently, despite the decree of Cyrus, thousands chose to remain in Chaldea. Apparently, not many more than fifty thousand ever returned to the Land of Promise.

Fortunately Israel's overcoming of the trials of the way before them did not depend on the peoples' strength alone. God's unlimited might would be placed at their aid also:

> When the poor seek for water but there is none,
>   And their tongue is dry from thirst,
> I, the Lord, will respond to them.
> . . . .
> I will open rivers upon bare heights,
>   And make springs in the valleys.
>
> —Isaiah 41:17–18[1]

God would cause even nature itself to cooperate for the good of those who would trust and follow him. In essence, what he was going to do for those who were faithful would be an evidence to all men that he was with Israel and would deliver her.

2. The Reassurance Provided (41:20)

All the phenomenal help of Jehovah to Israel was to have its particular purpose: "That they may see, and know, and consider, and understand together, that the hand of the Lord hath done this, and the Holy One of Israel hath created it."

Note the impressive verbs used: "see," "know," "consider," "understand." The evidence of God's guidance would be so comprehensive and compelling that no one could conclude that Israel's deliverance arose from any other source than God's grace.

II. THE GRACIOUS MISSION OF GOD'S SERVANT (42:1–12)

If there was still lurking in any mind the idea that God had chosen the people of Israel because they were better than or superior to others, such false thinking would now forever be corrected. They had been chosen for a purpose. God saw in Israel, despite all of her shortcomings, a people who through discipline could become the channel of his redeeming grace to the nations.

1. *The Mission Defined and the Method Disclosed* (42:1–3)

Chapter 41 dwells largely on the nature of God: his power, his supernatural deliverance, his incomparable greatness, his universal dominion. At this point in the prophecy a turn is made. The focus of the message at the time it was delivered fell upon God's servant people. Looking at the message from our Christian viewpoint, the focus seems to be clearly on the Servant who is Messiah and Redeemer, Jesus Christ.

Not only are men called upon to *behold* God's chosen Servant, they are called to witness the mission on which this Servant is sent: "He shall bring forth judgment to the Gentiles."

The Servant would not come with a spectacular message or a loud proclamation, but with restrained, calm, and serene authority (Matt. 3 : 17). He would be gentle with the weak and tender with the infirm: "A bruised reed shall he not break, and the smoking flax shall he not quench."

From the Christian perspective, we see clearly the quiet impressiveness of Jesus' teachings and the amazement of the people as they listened to him. "He taught them as one having authority, and not as the scribes" (Matt. 7 : 29). Matthew connected the prophetic thought with the work of Christ: "That it might be fulfilled which was spoken by Esaias [Isaiah] the prophet, saying, Behold my servant, whom I have chosen; my beloved, in whom my soul is well pleased: I will put my spirit upon him, and he shall shew judgment to the Gentiles. He shall not strive. . . . A bruised reed shall he not break, and smoking flax shall he not quench, till he send forth judgment unto victory. And in his name shall the Gentiles trust [hope]" (Matt. 12 : 17–21).

2. The Extent of the Mission Stated (42 : 4,6)

It is written in Isaiah: "He shall not fail nor be discouraged, till he have set judgment in the earth." Matthew understood this latter phrase to mean "till he send forth judgment unto victory," which is the same idea.

Both the prophet and the Gospel agree that Gentiles also were to be the object of the Servant's mission. The significance of inclusion of Gentiles in the statement in Isaiah (and of course in the New Testament, too) must not be overlooked. The covenant God gave his Chosen People is "for a light of [to] the Gentiles" (literally, to the nations). To this also, Isaiah 43:10 adds that the Israelites are to be his "witnesses" to these nations. The message of the grace of God must be shared by those who are its recipients.

3. The Power for the Mission Provided (42:5)

That which was to be the mission of God's Servant would require strength beyond what is normally given. But he who created the whole cosmos and crowned his work with the making of man would provide help for the task he assigned. The prophet heard the word of God assuring him, "I . . . will hold thine hand, and will keep thee." A more touching and reassuring promise would be difficult to imagine.

4. The Effect of the Mission Outlined (42:7)

Here is stated almost the same objective of the mission of God's Servant as recorded in Isaiah 61:1–2. His would be a ministry of compassion to men, bringing release from every form of bondage.

5. The Whole Earth to Be Affected (42:10–12)

He, whose name is above every name and whose glory can be shared by no other, is he who also will reveal "new things" which were soon to come to pass. God foreknew these "new things" and was now revealing them to the prophet, possibly long before they came to pass.

What God planned to do for Israel in that day, and through his people, called for a new song unto the Lord. It deserved to be upon every lip. "Let them give glory unto the Lord, and declare his praise in the islands" (v. 12). Ultimately the ends of the earth, including coastlands, would have cause to be affected by this new song and ought to be a part of it.

Edward Perronet's lines in "All Hail the Power of Jesus' Name" express the thought of the prophet:

> Let every kindred, every tribe,
> On this terrestrial ball,
> To Him all majesty ascribe,
> And crown Him Lord of all.

But who is the Servant to whom the prophet refers? The reference at the time of writing may have been to Israel as the Chosen People. God had called the nation not only as sons, but also to fill a servant's role. This purpose had been made clear from the time of Abraham. Israel was to be God's channel of blessing to all people. To fulfil this task, the people were to be his witnesses. Still more, through their race—or more exactly through the "seed" of Abraham—God's climactic work of redemption would be wrought.

Once again, looking from the Christian perspective, we see the Servant emphasis in the prophecy as reaching its highest fulfilment in him who said: "I came down from heaven, not to do mine own will, but the will of him that sent me" (John 6:38). Christ alone has truly become the "light" of all nations. "In him was life; and the life was the light of men. . . . [He is] the true Light, which lighteth every man that cometh into the world" (John 1:4–9).

Harrelson, in summing up the Servant idea in the prophecy, wrote that the prophet "sees in the life of Israel itself the quiet working of Yahweh's purpose. Even now, in her punishment for her own sins, Israel is bearing the sins of many." He later properly admits,

"The fulfillment of his [the prophet's] prophecy, from the viewpoint of Christian faith, comes in Jesus of Nazareth." [2]

III. GOD'S REDEEMING AND RESTORING LOVE (43:1-4)

The great guarantee of God's all-sufficient grace lay not in what Israel had done, but in what God had done and is doing.

1. *Further Reason for Removal of Fear* (43:1)

God himself who created Israel, to whom Israel thus rightfully belonged, and who "formed" them as a people, braced their faltering faith with his divine entreaty: "Fear not." But that call to confidence is based on a history which cannot and must not be forgotten:

> Fear not, for I have redeemed you;
> I have called you by name,
>   you are mine.
>   —RSV

What a triad of assurances this is!

Not only had God redeemed or ransomed Israel, as a slave is bought and set free; but he had also called her. That call was personal. "I have called you by name, you are mine," (RSV) he affirmed.

Lest Israel still think she was a "worm," cast off and forgotten, God added assuringly, "Thou art mine." Though they were unworthy and had forfeited any right to his mercy, the people were yet "precious in his sight." They were his own possession.

The New Testament reminds us that God is concerned about us personally. Jesus said, "The very hairs of your head are all numbered" (Matt. 10:30).

2. The Trials Which Afford No Unendurable Test (43:2)

Israel belonged to God, as do the redeemed of every age. His presence was to be with her and his help constantly available. Yet she was not to assume that she would be delivered from all perils and trials. This lesson was a hard one for Israel to learn. It is equally difficult for God's people of this century. We are prone to think that because one is a Christian he should be delivered from suffering and sorrow. But such a deliverance would be contrary both to the natural laws of the world and to our own good. That Israel was to pass "through the waters," "the rivers," and even "the fire" in her future course is not denied. It may even be inferred by the phrase, "when thou passest," that such experiences would be inevitable. But she would pass *through* these trials, not be consumed by them. The Christian can face his suffering and trials with equal assurance.

3. The Preciousness of God's People in His Sight (43:3-4)

One of the most astounding revelations contained in the Scriptures is set down in this section. It was made in connection with the prophet's attempt to help Israel see how much God was willing to do to deliver her. Using a term understood by people accustomed to the paying of ransoms, the prophet revealed that God would give, as it were, Egypt and other kingdoms also to Cyrus as a ransom price for liberating his people. The prophet was forecasting the conquests Cyrus would make in his rise to world dominance and to the position from which he would free the Jews. In painting this picture before their eyes, he wrote the inspiring and moving revelation:

> Because you are precious in my eyes,
>   and honored, and I love you,
> I give men in return for you,
>   peoples in exchange for your life.
>
> —Isaiah 43 : 4, RSV

It is a mystery that man, despite his unworthiness, can be "precious in the eyes" of God and honored and loved by him. Yet this fact is affirmed not only here, but most of all in the death of Christ in man's behalf. "The cross pays man no compliment," it has been wisely observed, "unless it be this, that God considered man worth dying for." How can men become thus precious in God's eyes? How but by the grace of God?

---

[1] Elmer A. Leslie, *Isaiah* (Nashville: Abingdon Press, 1963), p. 147.

[2] Walter Harrelson, *Interpreting the Old Testament* (New York: Holt, Rinehart, and Winston, 1964), p. 250.

5

GOD'S MAJESTY AND POWER

To BEHOLD a towering peak of the Alps or the Andes or to stand before the Himalayan giant, Mount Everest, lifting its craggy heights to 29,141 feet, is to be filled with wonder and awe. How much greater is man's amazement when he beholds the glory of the Lord God Almighty. Compared to him, even colossal mountains become as footstools!

Isaiah enables one again and again to view the unforgettable splendor and glory, the majesty and power of the living God.

I. HIS INCOMPARABLE GREATNESS (43:11–13; 44:6–8)

God emphatically affirms through the prophet his own uniqueness, saying: "I, even I, am the Lord; and beside me there is no saviour."

The Lord alone is God, the prophet speaking for God asserted; and thus he alone is man's Saviour. There is none to be compared to him. One writer has said that the above verse "is monotheism at its most intense pitch."

But the true and unique nature of God was not found by speculation. It was revealed through experience. God "declared," that is, by revelation he made known his nature and purpose. He also "saved." And he intended that Israel was never to forget this historic fact.

History has recorded for all ages to witness the unquestioned deliverance God effected for his people. Israel had been brought out of bondage through the power and supreme authority of God alone. Thus, he only was their Saviour. Other than God, there was none to help, absolutely no one to save. Indeed, except for him there is still no Saviour! This is the point of the proclamation here. Those who have been saved by him are "witnesses" to this truth (43:12).

Not only had God declared that he was Israel's Saviour, but he had shown it (proved it). The proof was not in a theory or even in a theological statement, however logically set forth, but in a historical experience. "Therefore you are My witnesses, says the Lord, that I am God" (43:12, Amplified).[1] People who have been redeemed and know it cannot help being witnesses. They truly have something to tell.

Nor does the case for God's greatness rest solely upon the proclamation of it or the historic record of his saving work (v. 13). It rests instead upon the past, present, and permanent nature of his being: "Yea, before the day was I am he." This statement about the eternal being and majesty of God recalls the great "I AM" given to Moses at the burning bush (Ex. 3:14). These declarations evidently have reference to God's self-existence and eternal being.

As God is the eternal Lord and Saviour, he works and none can hinder or reverse his purposes. It was clearly evident from Israel's experience that God had power greater, for example, than that of a mighty Egyptian monarch. He could divert the course of history and, as he did in the defeat of Egypt at the Red Sea, cause nature itself to serve his cause. Surely no man or man-made god has power to nullify his course of action or to reverse his plans (44:7).

What a strong tonic this sort of preaching must have been to a people who had almost totally lost hope! What they needed to discover was not that their God was too small for their needs and emergencies, but that their faith in him was too limited. God was able to fulfil his promises then, however impossible the prospect seemed. He was as able to deliver his people out of Babylonian captivity as he had been to deliver them formerly out of Egyptian bondage. His own people must believe this obvious truth. But the context reveals (vv. 8–10) that God wanted the heathen nations also to discover the fact. (See v. 9 especially.) He, therefore, subpoenaed or summoned the nations to appear also as witnesses to what he was about to do (v. 11). The whole world must come to see God's incomparable greatness and to know of his limitless power to save. Truly, "besides God there is and will be no other god." [2]

Certain proofs of God's greatness are also set down in this passage: his infallible foreknowledge and revelation in advance of the course of events yet to take place (43:12a); his power to carry out his purpose, as history affirms (43:13b).

The phrase, "I will work, and who shall let [hinder] it?" is perhaps better translated "I work, and who shall undo it?" No one possesses the power to reverse the course God's work has taken or to nullify what he has done. If this was true of the past, can any less be expected of the future?

How appropriate is the reminder, "Thus saith the Lord the King of Israel, and his redeemer the Lord of hosts; I am the first, and I am the last; and beside me there is no God" (44:6). To most Christians, this verse will have a familiar ring. It is indeed almost the same idea as found in Revelation. (See 1:8,11; 22:13.) The meaning in each case seems to be that the Lord is the Eternal One and the only God there is. Not only are the gods man has conceived no rivals to him; they are not even to be recognized at all. He alone is eternal—the first and the last—and he alone is God. "Beside me there is no God." This one God of all creation is King of Israel, and more; he is man's redeemer. Israel's sins, not God's lack of power to save or his indifference, had been the cause of the peoples' bondage. But through his grace God had redeemed them. This was reason enough not only for them not to be afraid, but also for them to acknowledge to all men the unsurpassed greatness of their God.

> Who is like me? Let him proclaim it,
>   let him declare and set it forth before me.
> Who has announced from of old the things to come?
>   Let them tell us what is yet to be.
>   —Isaiah 44:7, RSV

The people of God were now given solid reason to heed the assurance, "Fear ye not, neither be afraid."

The literal rendering of the above phrase is "be not distracted with fear." Weakened faith and growing fear are bad enough in themselves, but they produce something worse: distraction and inner confusion. Thus, they undo a man and lead to his defeat.

"Is there a God beside me?" Isaiah understood the Lord to ask. This is a question which still rolls down across the centuries, a question which no one—historian, philosopher, or any other—has been able to answer in any way but with a resounding *no*.

"There is no God; I know not any," is more literally rendered, "There is no rock; I know not any" (44:8). The idea of God as a rock has old rootage. (See Deut. 32:4,31; Psalm 18:2.) The New Testament affirms that Christ is the "rock," the one foundation which is eternally secure (Matt. 21:42–44; 1 Cor. 3:11; 1 Peter 2:8). What foundation or hope of security can man find elsewhere in this changing and uncertain world than in the God who has revealed himself in Christ? Truly, the only proper answer to the question asked is "I know not any." There is no other Rock save that which is found in the Eternal.

II. His Superiority over Other Powers (44:9–20; 45:9–12,22–23)

1. *The Folly of Idolatry* (44:9–20)

It has already been pointed out that most of the book of Isaiah is written in poetic form. The passage under study, however, is in prose. And what masterful prose it is! This passage deals vividly with the folly of making and worshiping idols. Idol makers, it declares, are "nothing." Their work is vain and useless. It is "confusion, chaos and worthlessness" (Amplified).

Leslie said of this passage that the prophet here, in 44:9–20, "gives utterance to the most elaborate and remorseless satire on the folly of idols contained in the Old Testament." [3] Idols are made, the reasoning seems to run, by the frail hands of men. It is inferred that since the maker is superior to that which is made, the idols must perforce be weaker than even the weak hands which formed them.

The description of how the tree is grown and the wood fashioned for an idol is graphic. But the irony of the prophet reached even greater heights than his descriptive powers as he pointed out that with parts of the same tree, a man cooks his food and warms himself. Then, with the residue, he makes a god to worship. Modern men smile at such naiveté. But at the very moment we begin to smile over the stupidity of such self-deception, we are pricked by an uneasy realization that we may do but little better ourselves.

Too many of us still give our primary concern, even allegiance, to things made by our hands—our houses, our clothes, our boats, our automobiles, our money. The idols we fashion for ourselves may be more subtly and less consciously conceived than the ancients', but they are no more worthy of worship than was the hewn stump of a tree. This we should not forget. Nor should we forget that millions are still worshiping idols not greatly unlike those to which the prophet referred. The idol, or god, factories are still doing a thriving business in many nations. Unless Christians do a better job of getting the gospel to these nations convincingly, uncounted millions will never know any other hope than the imaginary security afforded by their superstitious worship of gods made with human hands.

All around the Israelites in Babylon, as in most of the rest of the world of that day, the making and worship of idols was common. And because their captors seemed to fare better than they, many Hebrews must have been almost persuaded that the gods of the people about them were stronger than the God of their fathers. Perhaps some Israelites were making idols, as their fathers had done before them. The power of the prophet's irony surely must not have been lost upon most of the people. And they must have realized the truth in his perceptive disclosure of the pathetic poverty of such religious rites as idol worship afforded. Yet some of them seemed not to have heeded the prophet's warning. This is suggested by the statement, "He feeds on ashes; a deluded [self-deceived] mind has led him astray, and he cannot deliver himself or say, 'Is there not a lie in my right hand?' " (44:20, RSV). A free translation might be, "Is not this thing I am holding in my right hand a deception?" Man persistently deceives himself when he ignores God and finds the object of his worship in something other than the Eternal God.

2. The Futility of Striving with God (45:9–12)

The chapter out of which this passage is taken is remarkable in many ways. It begins, "Thus saith the Lord to his anointed, to Cyrus, whose right hand I have holden . . . I will go before thee . . . and I will give thee the treasures of darkness. . . . For Jacob my servant's sake, and Israel mine elect, I have even called thee by thy name: I have surnamed thee, though thou hast not known me" (45:1–4). Though Cyrus was not his follower, God had chosen to use the Persian to bring about the release of God's people from captivity. This was not the first time in history, nor has it been the last, when God made use of nonbelievers to carry out his plans. As Lord of history and sovereign of the universe, he is at liberty to chose his own ways to bring about accomplishment of his purposes. How futile it is then for men to fight against him. This is the essence of the warning and invitation expressed in 45:9–12. The prophet reasoned that it would be as logical for the clay to argue with the potter regarding the forming of a vessel, or for a child in conception to protest to its father and mother about its birth, as for man to resist or try to thwart God's plans. The prophet used powerful metaphors to help men understand and acknowledge the greatness of the Ruler of the universe.

The Jews in Chaldea likely had many questions regarding man's seemingly successful resistance of God. In our day, we have doubts because of the success of communism or other groups who defy God. We ought to remember how God ultimately worked out his own purposes through a ruler who did not know him. Though we cannot see it now, one day we may see breathtaking evidence that even now God is moving in history to achieve his purpose for man.

3. *The Hope of All the Earth* (45 : 22–23)

In the remainder of chapter 45, a magnificent promise to Israel is set down, and a universal invitation is extended. Some think that Isaiah 45 : 14–17 represents the reaction and testimony not of Israel, but of surrounding nations as they looked upon what God would do and was doing for Israel. These hold that the phrase "thou art a God that hidest thyself" would be the amazed confession of other nations at what God was shortly to do for Israel. It could also have referred to Israel's past feeling. Many Jews thought God had really gone into seclusion!

But, in these verses, salvation was assured Israel. And the deliverance in view was to be effected through Cyrus, one who did not even worship Israel's God. Cyrus would come at last to sense that a power not his own was working in him. He would come to know that

Israel's God is the one true Eternal God of all the earth.

The prophet foresaw that pagan religions would finally collapse and the nations would confess that the God he proclaimed is the only God. "The only God is the God of Israel, a Savior. He who is *hidden* in the shroud of mystery is *known* by the salvation he has wrought for his people." [4] Thus the God that "hidest" himself will reveal himself. The splendor of the ethical and moral conquest which was to be made for and in Israel would be beheld by all nations. This would lead them to seek knowledge of God through Israel.

Was more in view here than Israel's deliverance from Babylonian captivity and her success in becoming the means through whom the true God of all the earth was to be known? It would seem so from what follows: "Look unto me, and be ye saved, all the ends of the earth: for I am God, and there is none else." This message extends a universal invitation to, and offers hope for, all the earth. This was truly good tidings for all the nations. It is entirely possible that this very passage from Isaiah could have been in the mind of Paul as he wrote Philippians. Observe his use of almost the exact words of the last part of 45:23 which reads "That unto me every knee shall bow, every tongue shall swear." Now, note Paul's words: "And that every tongue should confess that Jesus Christ is Lord, to the glory of God the Father" (Phil. 2:11). Thus Paul proclaimed the ultimate and universal victory of Christ. What was declared by Isaiah was to be fulfilled in Christ.

III. HIS PROMISE AND POWER TO KEEP (49:8–16)

Similar emphases to those we have already discovered in chapters 43–45 are also found in the chapters which follow. Chapter 46 opens, for instance, with the beautiful and touching assurance to "Jacob, and all the remnant of the house of Israel," that God who had carried them from birth would bear them even to their old age as a father carries a frail or helpless child. Babylon, which had taken Israel into captivity, would itself be humiliated and destroyed (47:1–9).

The suffering which Israel had borne had been as a refining process (48:10). It had come because God's own character required him to act in judgment. Yet his judgment was tempered with mercy (48:9). Tested in the furnace of affliction, Israel would now be all the stronger. Indeed, she would profit from this instruction; it is suggested: "I am the Lord thy God which teacheth thee to profit" (48:17). God, furthermore, had a glorious purpose for her. God's servant was to be a light to the nations, that the salvation of God may extend to all peoples of the earth.

But how could such a high purpose be fulfilled by such a feeble people? Israel was now despised—perhaps had even pitied and despised themselves (49:7). The way back to Zion at best would be a trying one. The heat and the ruggedness of the route would be hard to endure. But God knew the peoples' anxiety and had already thought of their needs. He thus assured Israel through the prophet not only that he had answered their prayers in advance—"In an acceptable time have I heard thee"—but also that he had determined to guard them, to reinstate them as his covenant people, and to establish them in the Land of Promise. He would prepare the way in the mountains for them and provide food even there so that they should not be hungry and water that they need not thirst. He would so care for them that the burning heat would not strike them (9–11). But Israel needed to remember that God expected his people to be a light to all nations.

Note that the promise in verses 10 and 11 seems to be echoed in Revelation 7:16. As we look back on this prophecy, we can know that God's promises were more far-reaching than the prophet or his hearers likely knew at the time.

Such an assurance as was provided fearful Israel was cause for highest praise and greatest rejoicing. It was indeed enough to make heaven and earth resound with praise: "Sing, O heavens; and be joyful, O earth; and break forth into singing, O mountains: for the Lord hath comforted his people, and will have mercy upon his afflicted" (49:13).

From her position as a captive people, Israel was apparently not disposed to rejoice. Her faith was still too weak to accept, at face value, the promises which had been given. She could only recall the pains and privations of the past. Her reaction is seen in the statement: "But Zion said, The Lord hath forsaken me, and my Lord hath forgotten me."

How striking it is that in a moment when God was about to do a marvelous thing for them, the people of Israel strongly believed he had forsaken them—indeed, that he had utterly forgotten them. But for God to forget and forsake his people is as impossible as for a mother to forget her own baby in her arms (49:15). Indeed, a mother might forget, but God could not. His awareness of his children is so deep and so sure that it is as though he had graven or tattooed them on his hands where they would ever be before his eyes (49:16). A stronger assurance of the unfailing care and unlimited help of the Lord is hardly conceivable. The assurance came solely, of course, because of the grace and compassion of God, not the merit of the people.

[1] *The Amplified Old Testament* (Grand Rapids, Mich.: Zondervan Publishing House, 1962), p. 580.

[2] Herbert G. May and Bruce Metzger, ed., *The Oxford Annotated Bible* (New York: Oxford University Press, 1962), p. 875.

[3] Leslie, *op. cit.*, p. 159.

[4] *The Interpreter's Bible* (Nashville: Abingdon Press, 1956), V, 530.

6

FOREGLEAMS OF CHRIST

THE WRITERS of the New Testament profoundly believed that in Christ the great messianic promises of the Old Testament found supreme fulfilment. From their viewpoint, Isaiah is rich with material concerning the Messiah. This chapter will deal with material which should be specifically noted.

I. HIS NAME (7:10–16)

Few Old Testament verses are better known than Isaiah 7:14: "Therefore the Lord himself shall give you a sign; Behold, a virgin shall conceive, and bear a son, and shall call his name Immanuel."

The records of both Matthew and Luke support the belief that this prophecy had specific fulfilment in the birth of Christ. Matthew said of the angel's prediction to Joseph, "Now all this was done, that it might be fulfilled which was spoken of the Lord by the prophet, saying, Behold, a virgin shall be with child, and shall bring forth a son, and they shall call his name Emmanuel, which being interpreted is, God with us" (Matt. 1:22–23). Luke, a physician, gives convincing evidence that Isaiah's prophecy had reference to the miraculous birth of Jesus (Luke 1:26–35).

The context of the verse in question indicates that the prophecy was given during the reign of Ahaz when

Jerusalem was suffering pressure from a confederacy formed by Rezin, king of Syria, and Pekah, son of Remaliah, king of Israel (2 Kings 16:5; 2 Chron. 28:5-6; Isa. 7:1). The fall of the Northern Kingdom, then called Israel, had, of course, not as yet taken place.

Ahaz, to protect himself against Rezin and Pekah, seems already to have sought an alliance with Tiglath-pileser III, king of Assyria, sometimes called Asshur, and was depending on that alliance for needed help. Isaiah was vigorously opposed to the alliance. He was convinced that the alliance indicated Ahaz was placing greater confidence in the assistance of a heathen king than in the help of God. The prophet spoke for God as he challenged Ahaz to believe that if only the people would turn to him, God would deliver Judah out of her crisis. He called upon Ahaz to ask for a sign from God as a guarantee that God's assistance would be given. The king was offered an almost unlimited scope for his request: "Ask thee a sign of the Lord thy God; ask it either in the depth, or in the height above." The request could be as deep as Sheol or as high as heaven (v. 11). Thus, the prophet emphasized the universal authority and power of God, with an implied contrast to the weakness of even the most powerful king.

Feigning a reverence he did not possess, Ahaz refused to ask for a sign. Perhaps he thought he already had something going in his alliance with Assyria that was more certain than anything the prophet could promise. Isaiah had at first addressed Ahaz, using the phrase "The Lord *thy* God." When Ahaz refused to ask for a sign, the prophet replied with another phrase of significance, "Will ye weary *my* God also?" Here it is not the phrase "thy God" but "my God" which Isaiah employed. When Ahaz refused to act upon the authority of God, he not only disobeyed God, he also rejected him as his God. Isaiah then no longer spoke to Ahaz of "thy God."

But Isaiah gave Ahaz a sign anyway. The sign was that a child would be conceived whose name would be Immanuel. Before this child would be old enough to discern right from wrong, something worse than the threat of Rezin and Pekah would befall the land. Indeed, these kings, whom the prophet likened to ends of two smoking sticks or wooden pokers, were doomed to fail (vv. 4-9). Assyria, to whom Ahaz had turned for help, would both destroy Ephraim (the Northern Kingdom) and bring vast affliction also upon Judah. Subsequent developments, it should be remembered, proved the grim and tragic accuracy of Isaiah's prophecy (v. 17).

The sign given to Ahaz has been interpreted a number of ways. These range all the way from the view that a son was shortly to be born either to Isaiah or, more likely, to an unmarried daughter of Ahaz, to the view expressed in the Gospels of Matthew and Luke that it was a prediction of the birth of Christ. Some think it not impossible that both an early and a more distant fulfilment of the prophecy was included.

One reason why many hold to the idea that the reference was to a birth of special significance soon to take place is that the Hebrew word which is translated "virgin" (*almah*) refers literally to a young woman who might or might not be a virgin. This view is counterbalanced for many by Matthew's quotation of the passage, in which he uses the word "virgin" (Greek, *parthenos*). From Matthew's use of the Isaiah passage,

Christians have seen Isaiah 7 : 14 to be a reference to the coming of Jesus. The import of the verse in both places is the name given the child: Immanuel, "God is with us." It is important that we not permit this truth to be lost in theological debate.

The revelation regarding the birth of the child who was to bear the remarkable name Immanuel was strikingly given to Ahaz and the people of Judah at a time of grave spiritual declension and peril. It was evidently provided as an assurance of the presence of God in their midst even in their suffering and danger. The name would be a living evidence that the God of their fathers was still not only with them but was continuing to bring to pass his purposes in and through Israel. Though Ahaz had hardened his heart against God and had patently rejected the prophet's appeal, God had not forsaken his people. Deliverance of the remnant who trusted him, whatever happened to Ahaz and his house, was certain.

Looking back now upon this marvelous assurance in the light of the New Testament, we must interpret the prophecy as having its highest fulfilment not in an event of Ahaz's day, but in the coming of him who is the Word that "became flesh and dwelt among us" (RSV). As the New Testament affirms, Christ truly is "God with us."

How near God was to Israel! Yet they seemed unable to believe then that this could be so. He was not only near but was "with" them. It is blessed to know that God, rather than making fleeting appearances, *dwells with us.* Through the incarnation he entered our very nature, becoming the God-man, that he might redeem us.

II. HIS ADVENT (40: 3–5)

Here we come to another statement familiar to all who know the New Testament. The language is almost identical, in fact, with that found in all four Gospels in reference to the coming of John the Baptist as a forerunner of Christ (Matt. 3: 3; Mark 1: 2–3; Luke 3: 4–6; John 1: 23). In Christian thought, therefore, the passage has been understood as being messianic in nature and as referring specifically to the ministry of John the Baptist in introducing Christ to the world.

The present passage occurs in the great message on comfort (Isa. 40) already examined in chapter 3. The original purpose of that message, as noted earlier, was to comfort Israel by giving her assurance that her affliction in Babylonian captivity was at an end. Under the reign of Cyrus, Israel's bondage was to be broken and the people were to be set free.

But, as Clyde T. Francisco has noted in *Introducing the Old Testament*, this passage contains more than an assurance to the exiles of divine mercy and deliverance. As we see it now, it pointed also, by implication if not directly, to the advent of Christ. Its ultimate and highest spiritual fulfilment came when John the Baptist prepared the way for Jesus to deliver mankind out of the captivity of sin. Whatever immediate fulfilment it had did not rule out the latter and the larger.

John the Baptist understood the prophecy to refer specifically to his own ministry in making preparation for the introduction of the Messiah. That introduction was not a mere announcement but a call upon men to prepare the way, by genuine repentance, for the coming of Christ. John understood his work of making straight a way for the Lord to be a spiritual task. Mighty and memorable was the preaching of John. But its greatest significance lay in the fact that it pointed to him who was mightier still, the one whom John proclaimed as "the Lamb of God, which taketh away the sin of the world" (John 1:29).

III. His Titles (9:1-7)

Although the passage mentioned above (Isa. 40:3-5) is thought to have had as its setting the fall, or anticipated fall, of Babylon around 539 B.C., 9:1-7 is related to a period many years earlier, just after the death of Ahaz. Hezekiah apparently was then king. Intrigue such as had been common earlier under Ahaz was still being perpetrated by ambitious rulers of the day. Isaiah, however, held high hope that through Hezekiah, a ruler more responsive to the will of God than his father, a new day was dawning.

Some think the passage under consideration may originally have been a poem composed by Isaiah for use in celebrating the accession of Hezekiah to the throne. It is known that Hezekiah in his earlier days was not only reverent toward God but attentive to the counsel of the prophet. Isaiah perhaps had great confidence that Hezekiah would lead the nation back to a closer relationship with God. That the prophet might have written a poem in honor of Hezekiah's accession to the throne does not, therefore, seem unreasonable.

The problem of interpreting the present passage, as suggested above, is that more than an earthly ruler was envisioned. For example, the clause in verse 6, "For unto us a child is born," may be related to the thought in Isaiah 7:14. It is the foundation for the hope expressed in this entire passage. An earlier statement, "The people that walked in darkness have seen a great light" (v. 2), was definitely understood by Matthew and apparently also by Luke to refer specifically to the ministry of Christ (Matt. 4: 14–16; Luke 2: 32).

Through the coming of the one of whom the prophet spoke, the dawning of a glorious day would be brought to pass. Though darkness and anguish had long fallen upon Judah, as a night which had no end (8: 22), a great light would in time break through the darkness. That light, history reveals, entered into the world when Christ was born.

According to Isaiah 9: 1, the lands of Zebulun and Naphtali were to be affected by that which was promised. Nazareth, interestingly, was located in the territory of Zebulun and Galilee in Naphtali. In these areas, Jesus began his public ministry. Who can calculate what his preaching and healing did to dispel the darkness of this region, as of all others he touched?

Again, as in previous instances noted, the immediate reference of the prophet could have been to the restoration which would follow the overrunning of the land by Tiglath-pileser and later by Nebuchadnezzar. But, as has been properly observed, "to Christian faith the great prophecy has had its fulfillment in the birth of Jesus of Nazareth." Kilpatrick goes on to say, "It is amazing how every detail of the song fits our case and meets our needs. Across the centuries it leaps; spoken to the despairing hearts of a handful of Jews more than twenty-five hundred years ago, it gives voice to the thanksgiving of all the sons of men of the great deliverance and a divine Savior. Timeless and universal, it is the song of the Redeemer and his kingdom." [1]

In this Redeemer, the prophet foresaw the breaking of the bondage which had fallen upon the people and the lifting of their yoke. The government would be upon the shoulders of this new ruler, and his name would be called: "Wonderful Counselor, Mighty God, Everlasting Father, Prince of Peace" (v. 6, RSV). Though universally sovereign, this king would be a blessed, merciful ruler. The names given the coming ruler emphasize his wisdom, absolute deity, eternal being, and his work as the Prince of peace. Jesus Christ is the only one in all the knowledge of man to whom these titles can properly and fully apply.

In the Hebrew text there is no comma between "wonderful" and "counsellor." This means that there are really four, not five, titles given to the child who is to be born. The last of these, "Prince of Peace," has become universally familiar as a name for Jesus. The Hebrew word for peace used here refers to more than the end of war. It suggests a condition of rich, harmonious, and positive well-being. The idea, therefore, is consistent with that which the New Testament shows to be the consequence of the work of Christ in the human heart and in man's relationship to man. When Jesus truly becomes one's Lord and Saviour, this kind of peace not only becomes his personal possession but also his persistent pursuit in his relationship with others.

This prophecy under consideration further says, "Of the increase of his government and peace there shall be no end, upon the throne of David, and upon his kingdom, to order it, and to establish it with judgment and with justice from henceforth even for ever. The zeal of the Lord of hosts will perform this" (v. 7). Luke must have had this passage in mind when he quoted the proclamation of the angel to Mary (Luke 1:32-33). Christ came, of course, through the line of David. The kingdom he was to establish, unlike that of David or any successor of David, is to have no end. It would be marked with both judgment and justice, or, as is better translated, his purpose would be "to uphold it with justice and with righteousness" (v. 7, RSV).

IV. HIS MISSION (61:1-3)

Christ himself is our best interpreter of this passage. At the synagogue in Nazareth, he opened the Scriptures to this very passage in Isaiah and having read it he declared, " 'Today this scripture has been fulfilled in your hearing' " (Luke 4:21, RSV). Thus, Jesus is our authority for concluding that the passage refers climactically to his own earthly mission. Because of his use of it, the passage has enduring meaning for the Christian.

The passage is a magnificent summary of the many-faceted ministry of our Lord while here in the flesh. The speaker in the passage is not identified, but it is inferred that he is the Servant elsewhere referred to in the prophecy. Paul reminded us that Jesus "stripped Himself [of all privileges and rightful dignity] so as to assume the guise and form of a servant [slave], in that He became like men and was born a human being" (Phil. 2:7, Amplified). In this glorious prophecy, we catch an early glimpse of God's stooping in Christ to meet our human need.

Jesus was supremely the "anointed" of the Lord (v. 1). To be anointed was to be set apart in a solemn way for a particular purpose. The first ministry predicted of him was, as Jesus affirmed, "to preach good tidings."

Here we come again upon the phrase "good tidings." The Amplified Version uses the word "Gospel" in translating "good tidings."

The phrase, "good tidings," is encountered earlier in Isaiah 40:9: "O Zion, that bringest good tidings." "This is the first occurrence of the word which, passing through the Greek of the LXX [Septuagint] and the New Testament [*euaggelizesthai*], has had so fruitful a ministry, as embodying the message of the gospel—Good-spell, glad tidings—to mankind. The primary meaning of the Hebrew word is *to make smooth*, or bright, and so to 'gladden.' " [2]

These good tidings which the divine messenger was to bring are to be borne to "the afflicted." This word may be translated also as "the poor" or "the meek." Did Jesus have the same thought in mind when he referred in the Beatitudes to the meek who will inherit the earth?

The next part of the mission of the one spoken of in the passage is "to bind up the brokenhearted." Here again we may well recall Jesus' saying, "Blessed are the poor in spirit, for theirs is the kingdom of heaven. Blessed are those who mourn, for they shall be comforted" (Matt. 5:3-4, RSV). Was there ever another who so relieved sorrow, who so sympathetically removed that which breaks human hearts?

"To proclaim liberty to the captives," as set forth in the prophet's description of the ministry of him who should come, possibly refers first to the freeing of the exiles. But we see in it the deeper liberation implied in Jesus' teaching: "If you continue in my word, you are truly my disciples, and you will know the truth, and the truth will make you free. . . . So if the Son makes you free, you will be free indeed" (John 8:31–36, RSV).

"The year of the Lord's favor" (61:2, RSV) is contrasted with the "day of vengeance" which the people had already experienced. The contrast perhaps signifies the mercy God would bestow upon those faithful to him. In the symbolic sense, the great "year of the Lord's favor" dates from the birth, death, and resurrection of Jesus Christ.

It is to be noted that Jesus' quotation of the passage under examination, as given in Luke, ended with the first part of this verse. The prophet went on to hold out assurance for Zion that the comfort God would bestow upon his people would be forever enduring and his favor unceasing. Fulfilment of this promise reached its greatest heights, too, not in the return of the captives from Babylon, but in the glory that came to Zion through the gift of the Messiah.

V. His Relation to Israel (11:1–9; 4:2–6)

One of the most familiar and greatly loved passages in Isaiah is 11:1–9. The breathtaking promise it contains has been the inspiration and hope of multitudes across the centuries. The poetic metaphors used depict a time when peace will so completely reign that strife and enmity shall be no more. This glorious day of tranquility is to be brought about by him who will "not judge by what his eyes see, or decide by what his ears hear; but with righteousness he shall judge the poor, and decide with equity for the meek of the earth; and he shall smite the earth with the rod of his mouth, and with the breath of his lips he shall slay the wicked.

Righteousness shall be the girdle of his waist, and faithfulness the girdle of his loins" (vv. 3–5, RSV).

Who is it who will bring to pass the golden day of peace and righteousness predicted? The answer is in Isaiah's prophecy: "There shall come forth a shoot from the stump of Jesse, and a branch shall grow out of his roots. And the Spirit of the Lord shall rest upon him, the spirit of wisdom and understanding, the spirit of counsel and might, the spirit of knowledge and the fear of the Lord" (11:1–2, RSV). This prophecy refers evidently to the Messiah's advent. It sees him as coming from the line of David. The phrase, "the stump of Jesse," obviously means from the family of Jesse, David's father.

While the text emphasizes the royal lineage through whom the Messiah would come, it also reveals the relationship of the Messiah to Israel. Thus, it conforms to the promise given long ago to Abraham that through his "seed" all the world should be blessed. Though the Messiah promised was to come through David's royal line and in many respects was to be like him, he nonetheless was to be possessed of supernatural knowledge and power. The reign which he was to bring would transcend natural laws and boundaries. This is inferred in the figures of speech found, for example, in verses 6–8. These depict such phenomena as the wolf and the lamb lying down together and a suckling child playing over the hole of an asp.

The effect of the coming of the branch predicted in the above passages is a transformation of the people and of their entire circumstances. The transformation predicted could have been brought about only by supernatural power.

The great promise, "For the earth shall be full of the knowledge of the Lord, as the waters cover the sea" (11:9), is yet in process of fulfilment. It is amazing, despite all failures of the church and all the foibles of Christians, how far-reaching has been the penetration around the world of the ethical ideals and moral principles disclosed in Christ. Whether or not men accept Christ as Saviour and Lord, they are compelled to confess that through him has been disclosed the highest revelation of moral and ethical truth known to man. He alone has vanquished spiritual darkness. He alone offers hope for the moral transformation of the world.

The passage just noted (11:1–9) and the earlier passage concerning the birth of Immanuel (7:14) are among the most precious and inspiring in the Old Testament to Christians generally. In the coming of the Messiah predicted by the prophet, the hope not of Judah alone but of all the world is realized.

VI. His Rejection by His People (6:9–12)

In the first part of this great chapter, the immortal record of the call of Isaiah and of his work as a prophet are reverently and magnificently set down. But what was to be the effect of Isaiah's preaching? What would be the result thereafter of the ministry of the one who fulfilled all requirements of Messiah?

In Isaiah's case, the result of his work was clearly that people would largely turn a deafened ear. Israel was so wedded to her sins that Isaiah had to say to them: "Hear ye indeed, but understand not; and see ye indeed, but perceive not" (6:9).

Jesus indicated that Isaiah's prophecy included also a forecast of how men would respond to his own message: "Therefore speak I to them in parables: because they seeing see not; and hearing they hear not, neither do they understand. And in them is fulfilled the prophecy of Esaias" (Matt. 13:13–14). (See also Acts 28:26–27; 2 Cor. 3:14–15.)

It is interesting to note that Isaiah 6:10 in the Aramaic is reflexive or passive, and means that "their eyes, ears, and hearts have been closed by love of the material world. . . . God did not close their eyes, nor stop their ears. They had brought this upon themselves through their disobedience and transgression against God's law and his ways of life." [3]

It had been revealed to Isaiah that despite the hardness of heart of the people to whom he would minister, at least a remnant would be saved. The apostle Paul accepted this idea and interpreted it in his letter to the Romans. More than once he quoted from Isaiah as his authority for the reasoning he set forth in Romans 9–11.

VII. His Victory over Death (25:8; 26:19)

The immortal account in Isaiah 53 concerning the Suffering Servant will be reserved for attention in the next chapter. It may be said here that Christians have commonly held this chapter and its prelude in chapter 52 to refer to the sacrificial death of Jesus.

In chapter 25, which is a song of praise, Isaiah was led to speak in a remarkable way of the abolition of death itself. The death of death, it should be noted, was to occur "in this mountain," namely, on Mount Zion (25:6).

The vision given, as is true of so many others, may have had its immediate prospect of fulfilment to the mind of the prophet in what would be done to the enemies of Israel. These had long brought death and devastation upon Judah (v. 10). The power to bring death would be nullified. The prophet wrote that "he will swallow up death in victory; and the Lord God will wipe away tears from off all faces; and the rebuke of his people shall he take away from off all the earth: for the Lord hath spoken it" (25:8). This prophecy has had no complete fulfilment in history unless it be in Christ's death upon the cross. The apostle Paul evidently so understood the prophecy, as he seems to have gathered up the same thought in 1 Corinthians 15:54 where he said, "Then shall be brought to pass the saying that is written, Death is swallowed up in victory."

Concerning 25:8, one scholar has written: "Death itself and all sorrow and trouble will be taken away from the people of the earth (v. 8). For this we can all hope, for the Lord has decreed it." [4]

In Isaiah 26:19 there is the amazing statement, "Thy dead shall live, their bodies shall rise. O dwellers in the dust, awake and sing for joy!" (26:19, RSV). This statement, though poetic, comes as close as it could without actual use of the word to mention of the resurrection. Surely the words of the prophet suggest a general resurrection. Fitch remarks concerning the verse, "This is the most wonderful message yet recorded in this section of the prophecy. In the previous chapter the truth of immortality has been disclosed in the word 'He hath swallowed up death for ever' (25:8). But this goes even further. This is an emphatic statement of the resurrection of the body. Here is the precursor of the full intimation of the great Christian doctrine of immortality." [5]

As one glances over the many messianic concepts found in the prophecy of Isaiah and recalls the New Testament record of their fulfilment, he cannot help but be struck all the more by the amazing character of this marvelous book. He will be moved also to rejoice with profound gratitude and wonder over the incomparable and indestructible plan of God wrought out in history to redeem the world.

---

[1] *Interpreter's Bible, op. cit.,* 230.
[2] C. J. Ellicott, *Commentary on the Whole Bible* (Grand Rapids: Zondervan Publishing House), IV, 521.
[3] George M. Lamsa, *Old Testament Light* (Englewood Cliffs, N. J.: Prentice-Hall, Inc., 1957), p. 628.
[4] Wright, *op. cit.,* p. 66.
[5] Davidson, Stibbs, and Kevan, *op. cit.,* p. 581.

7

THE SUFFERING SERVANT

In Isaiah 53, Old Testament prophecy rises to its highest pinnacle. Its sublime grandeur reaches beyond adequate description. Its inspiration and power to move the soul are incalculable.

The chapter and its introduction in 52:13–15 come from that section of the prophecy which contains the well-known Servant passages of 40 to 55. In the fifteen verses which comprise this particular passage, the focus is upon the Suffering Servant. Is the Servant portrayed some unknown person, the prophet himself, or the nation personified? Most modern scholars seem to lean toward the latter view. Others strongly disagree, holding that the Suffering Servant could be none other than Jesus of Nazareth.

Though Israel was certainly destined to play a servant role in fulfilment of her mission, most, if not all, of what is said in the present context points not to a nation but to a person. There are many scholars who support the position that the passage refers to Israel, and they argue that Israel is referred to here as an individual. The problem with acceptance of this interpretation is that it poses a question no one has as yet been able to answer satisfactorily: Why is it that nowhere else in the Old Testament, or even in Hebrew thought, do we find the idea emphasized here of the innocent suffering vicariously for the guilty? Israel was never said elsewhere so to suffer for others, but only for her own guilt. In the present passage, though, the innocent is presented as suffering for the guilty.

Therefore, it is the conclusion of this writer that the only interpretation which appears to satisfy the facts in the passage and to be consistent at the same time with the rest of prophetic writings is that the Suffering Servant described here found ultimate fulfilment in the mission of our Lord. The passage pictures Christ's death upon the cross. The Suffering Servant is the suffering Saviour.

The passage under study has remarkable parallels with the whole earthly life of the Master, its main emphasis being upon that which would be fulfilled by what took place at Golgotha.

We are not to suppose that the prophet fully understood all that his marvelous words were foreshadowing as to the sufferings of Christ. The first task of the interpreter is to try to discover what the writer himself understood by his words. But as Christians, taking our cue from Christ himself in Luke 24:27 and Philip in Acts 8:35, we can see the justification of Sampey's words: "The New Testament application of this great prophecy to Jesus is not an accommodation of words originally spoken of Israel as a nation, but a recognition of the fact that the prophet painted in advance a portrait of which Jesus Christ is the original." [1]

I. HIS AFFLICTION AND EXALTATION (52:13–15)

With Isaiah 52:13 a totally new theme is introduced. What follows in 52:13–15 is, in effect, a summary of or an introduction to chapter 53.

1. His Wisdom and Triumph (52:13)

This verse appears to have its antecedent in 49:1–7, where the Servant of the Lord is described as being engaged in a unique mission as well as having a unique nature. Though some argue that the thought there, too, relates solely to Israel as a nation, or else to the work of the prophet, it seems more specifically to denote the Messiah. Of no other could all the things described there, as well as in the passage under study, really be true. The Servant, for example, who was to be "a light to the Gentiles" (49:6) and was to be despised and abhorred was also to be honored by kings and worshiped by princes (v. 7). Here a similar thought is expressed, except that both the wisdom of the Servant and his exaltation are emphasized. The Servant's exaltation, as verse 14 discloses, is to come through suffering and rejection. Yet he is to "glorify himself" (a literal translation of 49:3) among men and to be exalted among the nations. Could Christ have had this very prophecy in mind when he remarked before the crucifixion, "Now is the Son of man glorified, and God is glorified in him" (John 13:31)? Truly he did glorify himself forever when he laid down his life on Golgotha.

The phrase "my servant shall deal prudently" carries the idea not only of acting in wisdom but also of prospering or succeeding (see RSV). Jesus once declared, "When ye have lifted up the Son of man, then shall ye know that I am he, and that I do nothing of myself; but as my Father hath taught me, I speak these things" (John 8:28). The idea in the prophetic passage seems to relate impressively to what Jesus anticipated as the certain consequence of his crucifixion. Referring to the preaching of the cross, later Paul also spoke of "Christ crucified, . . . the power of God, and the wisdom of God" (1 Cor. 1:23-24).

2. *His Supreme Suffering* (v. 14)

From the victory and exaltation described in 52:13, the prophecy moves to a brief description of the suffering endured by the Servant of the Lord. The phrase used here—"as [or in the manner] many were astonished"—stands in contrast with the subsequent remark, "so shall he sprinkle [startle] many nations" (v. 15). The contrast emphasizes that to the very extent to which men were astounded and moved by the sight of the Servant's afflictions, so should they be astonished and stirred by the spectacle of his glory.

The afflictions to be borne by the Servant were of such depth and degree that they were "more than any man" had ever endured. Men would be astonished and filled with horror at the sight of his marred appearance and would be appalled by the agony that was heaped upon him. His form was to be so distorted that it would lose all likeness to that of a man. Strangely underlying this thought is the idea expressed earlier in verse 13 of the wisdom exercised by him who moves through and by means of such affliction to a place of eminence above all others.

3. *His Exaltation Among the Nations* (v. 15)

We have here what apparently is developed in a more expanded statement in 53:11-12. The triumph of the Suffering Servant would be so remarkable that even the leaders of nations would be struck with wonder at what they beheld. "Kings shall shut their mouths at him." They would be left speechless with amazement at the marvel unfolded before them.

Paul apparently gathered up the thought expressed here when in Romans he said, "As it is written, To whom he was not spoken of, they shall see: and they that have not heard shall understand" (Rom. 15:21).

The awe provoked in men as they beheld the victory of the Servant over the afflictions he innocently bore would stir in them reverence and silent wonder. They would be made to stand in amazement and to be dumb with awe as they beheld him who even from the depths of abjection was revealed as the source of their own redemption. Only of Christ in all history can such a remarkable saying be true. Even monarchs beholding his glory have often longed to doff their crowns and lay them at his feet. Indeed, men continue to "stand amazed in the presence of Jesus the Nazarene."

The word "sprinkle" found here in the King James Version should be translated "startle" (RSV). The wonder of the work of redemption which the Suffering Servant is to perform will be the literal astonishment not merely of many people but of the nations. Inexplicable amazement will seize upon all who contemplate what he has wrought. His suffering and his victory will be so clearly facts of history that men cannot ignore them: "For that which had not been told them shall they see; and that which they had not heard shall they consider." In his agony it could be said of him, "So marred from the form of man was his aspect that his appearance was not that of the Son of man" (a literal translation of v. 14). It must now, however, be confessed in the words of the hymn:

No mortal can with him compare
Among the sons of men;
Fairer is he than all the fair,
Who fill the heavenly train.

—Samuel Stennett

II. His Humiliation and Rejection (53:1-3)

Only the broad outlines of the suffering to be endured by the Servant of the Lord and the consequences of that suffering are set forth in the latter part of chapter 52. The grim details are to be pictured in chapter 53. And what awesome particulars they are. In truth, they are so full of pathos and so horrifying, and their consequence paradoxically so far-reaching, as to seem wholly incredible and to raise the cry, "Who hath believed our report?"

To the Jews who first heard it, the unfolded account evidently seemed incomprehensible. To many across the ages, the story has been beyond credibility. Yet experience and history have combined to establish its authenticity.

1. The Source of the Question (53:1)

"Who hath believed our report? and to whom is the arm of the Lord revealed?" Presumably it was the prophet speaking, though some think it was Israel. The "report" is the message being unfolded. The meaning of the question seems to be, "Who could have believed what we have heard?" The answer implied by the question is, "No one." What was being proclaimed seemed so incredible that it seemed likely that no one could ever accept it.

"To whom is the arm of the Lord revealed?" concerns the strength and power of the Lord God. Who has understood the greatness of his power or the strength of his "arm" sufficiently to recognize that God can certainly do what he has revealed through the prophet he will do?

2. The Strangeness of the Servant's Coming (53:2)

Any farmer knows that for a shoot to sprout from dry ground is unusual. The laws of nature require moisture in the soil for germination. The Servant here spoken of was to come from just such an unusual origin —"dry ground." Though he would spring up spectacularly as a shoot out of dry ground, he would grow thus unspectacularly and quietly as does a tender young plant.

This metaphor easily brings to the Christian's mind the remarkable paradoxes related to the birth and early life of Jesus. Except for the one instance in the Temple, Jesus apparently grew up so simply as to call no particular notice to himself. His lowly birth, the age in which he was born, and the condition of the nation, too, could not have offered less promise as a source from which the Lord of all the earth should come.

Though reference is made here to the same idea as expressed in 11:1 regarding the branch, a different emphasis is noted. There it was his lineage from the root of Jesse that was in view; here is noted the unpropitious and remarkable nature of his birth. The phrase "grow up before him" suggests his growing up before God; that is, with God's unusual attention centered upon him.

The Gospel of John relates this prophecy specifically to the work of Christ. Following Jesus' remarks about the death he would die (John 12:32–33), it is recorded: "But though he had done so many miracles before them, yet they believed not on him: That the saying of Esaias [Isaiah] the prophet might be fulfilled, which he spake, Lord, who hath believed our report? and to whom hath the arm of the Lord been revealed?" (John 12:37–38). In the Gospel the question is introduced, "Lord, who hath . . . ?" signifying that it was addressed to God. If this was the case, then the prophet must have asked the question.

3. The Failure of Men to See His Beauty (53:2b)

The sense of the clause "there is no beauty that we should desire him" appears to be, "There was nothing in him that we should have looked at or desired him." Men were not coerced to come to him by the splendor of his personal appearance. In physique Christ was no superman, no Adonis. Though there is evidence that he was strong and vigorous, he was much like other men. Men were often deeply moved by his personality, but he appeared to them as no Saul of Kish standing head and shoulders above others. One writer has said that the Son of God who would be accepted by men would have to be one who could be mistaken for an ordinary man.

4. The Response of Men to Him (53:3)

"He was despised and rejected . . . a man of sorrows, and acquainted with grief." These lines form one of the most touching arias in Handel's *Messiah*. They are among the most poignant in the Scriptures. Only in the scene of Jesus' actual trial and crucifixion is there anything more touching. They remain among the most descriptive terms ever used of our Lord's rejection by men.

The words "sorrows" and "grief" in the Hebrew literally mean pain and sickness. Christ was never said to have been sick, but the torture he bore as he took upon himself the burden of human iniquity and sin burned in him like a raging fever. The pain and sickness may be identified, therefore, with his vicarious suffering for our redemption.

The appearance of the Suffering Servant was so appalling as to cause men to hide their faces from him. "We hid as it were our faces from him." Sickened and repelled by the sight of his agony, especially upon the cross, or else disgusted by his appearance and contemptuous of him, men turn their faces. A more accurate rendering of verse 3 is "one from whom men hide their faces" (RSV). In the phrase "we esteemed him not," the prophet placed himself among the people. Possibly the meaning of the phrase is, as Luther suggested, "We estimated him at nothing." A possible translation would be, "He was despised, and we did not give him a thought."

III. His Vicarious Suffering (53:4–6)

In this stanza of the great poem, we come to the point at which those who insist the account of the Suffering Servant has only a corporate reference to Israel seem least convincing. Nowhere else, if it is true here, is there evidence in the Old Testament of Israel's suffering vicariously for other nations. It is difficult, therefore, to believe the meaning of this passage is to be so interpreted. Vicarious suffering is clearly portrayed in chapter 53. The prophet affirmed, "Surely he hath borne our griefs, and carried our sorrows." That the one described in the passage was suffering for others is obvious. The language allows no other interpretation. These haunting lines, in truth, involve us all. We cannot escape.

The phrases of the passage stand out in awesome and arresting vividness. They starkly judge us all. Yet, when considered together they comprise the most inspiring evidence to be found anywhere before the crucifixion of the amazing mercy and kindness of God toward sinful mankind. Note their sequence as well as their significance:

"Borne our griefs"
"Carried our sorrows"
"Wounded for our transgressions"
"Bruised for our iniquities"
"The chastisement of our peace was upon him"
"With his stripes we are healed"
"The Lord hath laid on him the iniquity of us all"

Several conclusions seem inescapable from the above assertions:

The suffering was vicarious.
The suffering was voluntary.
The suffering was in obedience to the Lord.
The suffering was for "us all."
The suffering was mediatorial; that is, it was to have the power of effecting peace and reconciliation.

The words "griefs" and "sorrows," as earlier noted (v. 3), carry the idea of pain and sickness. Matthew, following an account of the healing ministry of Christ, related the idea set forth by the prophet, saying: "That it might be fulfilled which was spoken by Esaias the prophet, . . . Himself took our infirmities, and bare our sicknesses" (Matt. 8:17).

"Yet we did esteem him stricken, smitten of God, and afflicted." The erroneous idea persisted for ages in Israel that leprosy and other grave illnesses were all judgments of God. The opinions of Job's comforters are instances in point. Holding the same view, many would mistake the voluntary humiliation and affliction of the Suffering Servant to mean that God was chastening him. On the contrary, though he was wholly obedient to God the Father and was entirely undeserving of the suffering he bore, he assumed it only that he might deliver men from it—that he might deliver *us* from it! *Our transgressions* and *our iniquities* were the cause of his agony.

"All we like sheep have gone astray." It is the tendency of sheep, when they have lost their way, to wander farther and farther from the fold, rather than to return to it. Men are like sheep in more than one respect. They have done worse, so the prophet declared. "We have turned every one to his own way" (v. 6). Such was, in time, to be the confession of repentant Israel. It has since been the necessary admission of all whose consciences have been awakened. Each, like the psalmist, has prayed: "I have gone astray like a lost sheep; seek thy servant; for I do not forget thy commandments" (Psalm 119:176). Peter reminded believers, "Ye were as sheep going astray; but now are returned unto the Shepherd and Bishop of your souls" (1 Peter 2:25). Christ becomes the Shepherd and Bishop of our souls because, as he said, he is "the good shepherd: the good shepherd giveth [layeth down] his life for the sheep" (John 10:11).

"The chastisement of our peace was upon him" is a sentence full of meaning. The sense of these words appears to be that the suffering he bore would lead to our peace and blessing. The mediatorial aspect of his affliction is revealed. The purpose of his suffering was to lead to peace and reconciliation and to every form of blessing.

"And with his stripes we are healed." This phrase brings us to the heart of the marvelous assurance that the Servant's suffering is adequate to meet our needs. Doubtless Peter had the prophet's remark in mind as he wrote, "Who his own self bare our sins in his own body on the tree, that we, being dead to sins, should live unto righteousness: by whose stripes ye were healed" (1 Peter 2:24). The idea is that of being made whole and its effect a continuous one. In this immortal declaration, both the wonder and lasting power of our salvation come more fully into view.

IV. HIS CONDEMNATION AND DEATH (53:7–9)

While one may have felt a foreshadowing of the cross and indications as to the reason for the Messiah's humiliation in earlier passages of Isaiah, death does not come fully into view until 53:7–9. The amazing vividness with which the language parallels the steps which led Jesus from Pilate's court to burial in Joseph's new tomb continues to be the wonder of every reverent reader.

Every reader of the Gospels will recall that Christ "opened not his mouth" in his trials before the high priest and Pilate, except when questions of his own identity were asked (Matt. 26:62–64; 27:12–14). Was Jesus consciously fulfilling the prediction made in

Isaiah in each of these experiences? Such patience and self-restraint, as indicated in the prophecy and as revealed by Christ, were not traditional among the Hebrews. Old Testament sufferers characteristically lamented their afflictions and often cried out in complaint against pain and injustice. The lament of great prophets like Jeremiah and Habakkuk, as well as the complaint of Job, will be easily recalled.

"He is brought as a lamb to the slaughter." The emphasis here is on the victim's silent submission. But the Christian reader will recall that Philip used this very passage with the Ethiopian eunuch "and preached unto him Jesus" (Acts 8:30–35). The title, "The Lamb of God," became a common New Testament term for reference to Christ. Peter evidently had the title in mind in the following remark, "But with the precious blood of Christ, as of a lamb without blemish and without spot" (1 Peter 1:19). The book of Revelation more than once expresses the same idea.

The phrase, "He was taken from prison and from judgment," is perhaps better translated, "By oppression and judgment he was taken away" (RSV). It could be rendered "by oppression and without justice was he taken." This phrase certainly describes what happened to Jesus Christ, for the gross miscarriage of justice in the trial of Jesus is a record of history.

One of the most difficult phrases to interpret in the whole passage is, "Who shall declare his generation?" Perhaps a more accurate rendering is, "As for his generation, who considered that he was cut off out of the land of the living, stricken for the transgression of my people?" (RSV). The prophet wondered who among his own people had given the slightest thought as to the reason for the suffering borne by the Servant of the Lord.

The harsh details of this suffering have been alluded to already, so they are only suggested here. Their appalling vividness and horror also have been portrayed previously and thus need not be repeated.

The last couplet of the stanza assumes that the death of the Suffering Servant has already taken place. His burial is now at hand. "And he [they] made his grave with the wicked, and with the rich in his death." The literal rendering of the text is "one [or they] assigned him a grave." More recent translations use "they." The meaning appears to be that he was buried as a criminal would have been and not with the honors due him. Verse 8 of this passage emphasizes that the nation had not recognized that the stroke which fell upon the Suffering Servant really should have fallen upon them. In verse 9, the emphasis is that although his burial was with the wicked, there was no guilt in him, only absolute purity.

Though the first part of verse 9 poses difficulties in interpretation, for the Christian the meaning of the second part cannot be mistaken. From the viewpoint of the crowd which cried for Christ's crucifixion, he was buried disgracefully and ingloriously. Yet the providence of God turned the tables on this human folly and provided that he should be buried "with a rich man"; that is, in a rich man's chosen and especially prepared tomb. The intentions of those who crucified him were thus reversed. He was buried gloriously and, perhaps, in a place of unusual beauty and appropriateness.

The Christian can read this stanza of the poem and

easily recall the events of the trial and death of the Servant of the Lord. The verses which follow provide a grand climax to that awful scene.

V. HIS SERVANTHOOD AND SATISFACTION (53:10–12)

In verse 6 we are told, "And the Lord hath laid on him the iniquity of us all." Now it is said, "Yet it pleased the Lord to bruise him; he hath put him to grief." Sampey has observed, "The Servant's death, far from being an accident, was in Jehovah's plan for human redemption." [2]

By the phrase "it pleased the Lord" is meant that God's purposes in behalf of man were thus to be fulfilled. It pleased him only in the sense that the course chosen was one of necessity in order that man might be redeemed and brought back into reconciliation with his creator. The Gospel's assurance, "For God so loved the world, that he gave his only begotten Son," provides the only adequate answer to the question as to why God permitted Calvary.

"When thou shalt make his soul an offering for sin" is better translated "When he makes himself an offering for sin" (RSV).

The Messiah became an eternally sufficient offering for sin. This was his vicarious suffering. The main point of the verse concerns the consequences of that suffering. "He shall see his seed, he shall prolong his days, and the pleasure of the Lord shall prosper in his hand." It was the purpose of the Lord to bruise him because of the goal he had in view. That purpose would be prospered in his hand. This idea recalls the one earlier emphasized and indeed the whole accent of 52:13–15. The meaning is that "his spiritual posterity shall be numerous." The host of those who have believed on Christ through the centuries are uncountable. Almost a billion people now confess him. Though there are those who speak glibly today of a "post-Christian era," faith inclines us to the Pauline view that one day every knee shall bow to him and every tongue confess him (Phil. 2:10–11).

The phrase "he shall prolong his days" suggests the resurrection and the Servant's endless life thereafter.

In verse 11, the Servant's own reaction to his suffering and humiliation is disclosed. Seeing the fruit of his "travail" in the turning of nations unto himself by it, he will feel amply compensated for the agony he bore.

"By his knowledge shall my righteous servant justify many" could be interpreted as referring either to the knowledge Christ possesses concerning the Father or to the knowledge men receive through faith in him. "By their knowledge of him shall many be justified" could be the meaning. Either interpretation is consistent not only with the text but with man's experience. Possibly the knowledge experientially gained through personal union with Christ is more in keeping with the point being made. It is also consistent with the New Testament affirmation: "And this is life eternal, that they might know thee the only true God, and Jesus Christ, whom thou hast sent" (John 17:3). Jesus himself seems to be interpreting the very point made in Isaiah in his immortal prayer the night before his crucifixion.

Plumtre thought the last phrase of verse 11, "for he shall bear their iniquities," is reemphasized to stress the "perpetuity of the atoning work." [3] In Hebrews we read, "Wherefore he is able also to save them to the uttermost that come unto God by him, seeing he ever liveth to make intercession for them" (Heb. 7:25). The statement in Hebrews is in keeping with the statement in verse 10, "He shall prolong his days."

The words "great" and "strong" in verse 12 extend the thought expressed in 52:13,15 respecting kings and rulers of the nations. Not only will the great and strong "divide" honor and glory with him, but they will surrender sovereignty to him. This glorious consequence will come about "because he hath poured out his soul unto death: and he was numbered with the transgressors; and he bare the sin of many, and made intercession for the transgressors." Christ himself saw his crucifixion as fulfilling this immortal prophecy (Luke 22:37).

Thus is concluded one of the best loved chapters in all the Bible. It is so vivid in detail that one could think its writer was a personal witness to the Saviour's trial and actually stood at the foot of the cross. This chapter is even more amazing when one considers that it was written centuries before the crucifixion by one whose purpose was to console and encourage an exiled people.

----

[1] *The Heart of the Old Testament* (Nashville: Broadman Press, 1922), p. 173.

[2] *Loc. cit.*

[3] Ellicott, *op. cit.*, p. 173.

8

THE GOOD NEWS OF SALVATION

GOOD NEWS! This is the distinctive theme of Isaiah 49:1 to 55:13. The good news is the certainty of salvation, the gladsome hope of redemption.

For the most part, Isaiah 49:1 to 55:13 is concerned with the redemption of captive Israel and the return of the exiles from Babylon to Jerusalem. But, as we have already seen in chapter 7, there are exceptions where the text seems to depart from, or at least to reach beyond, this theme. Certain portions appear to have a universal sweep. This is notably so in chapters 49, 52, and 55.

The prophet, using a pattern of thought similar to that of Hosea, spoke in 50:1 of the Lord as a husband and Israel as a faithless wife. He heard the Lord inquiring, "Where is the bill of your mother's divorcement, whom I have put away? or which of my creditors is it to whom I have sold you? Behold, for your iniquities have ye sold yourselves, and for your transgressions is your mother put away." Israel, like the unfaithful wife described in Hosea, had fallen into bondage by her sins. She had, in effect, sold herself into captivity. In her bondage she had no price with which to purchase her freedom, no power by which to obtain her redemption. She was powerless to extricate herself from her sinful state.

I. REDEMPTION WITHOUT PRICE (52:1–3; 55:1–2)

To Israel in her sad estate came the good news that redemption would be obtained for her without price. Such was the marvelous grace and kindness of God toward the sinful nation that though she had sold herself for "nothing" she would "be redeemed without money." Selling herself had brought her no gain. This was poignantly obvious. She was thus helpless to redeem herself. In her affliction, she had tended to think God (her "husband" in the present metaphor) had sold her. In other words, Israel was blaming God for her plight. This erroneous idea was countered by a reminder that God had gotten nothing out of the sale (the captivity of Israel), nor did he have any creditors to whom he owed anything. "Which of my creditors is it," he asked, "to whom I have sold you?" Of course, there was no answer.

Neither from Israel's earlier bondage in Egypt nor from her later oppression by Assyria or Babylon (52:4) had God gained anything. Indeed, he had only been blasphemed, and thus grieved; and Israel had been made to "howl" because of her afflictions (52:5).

But now those who had afflicted Israel and had given no compensation to her or to God must release her. This they would do, and without money or reward. No compensation was due them and none would be given them. The Babylonians must, and would, let Israel go without price. This was the will of God who yet cared for Israel despite her unworthiness.

Of course, though no price would be paid Babylon for Israel's freedom, the nation's ultimate redemption would be costly. It would require of God a price beyond comparison, the vicarious death of the Messiah. Peter would write centuries later, "You know that you were ransomed . . . not with perishable things such as silver or gold, but with the precious blood of Christ, like that of a lamb without blemish or spot" (1 Peter 1 : 18–19, RSV).

Though the invitation of God through Isaiah was first directed to Israel, it was intended apparently to embrace men everywhere. "Ho, every one that thirsteth," the prophet proclaimed, "come ye to the waters, and he that hath no money; come ye, buy, and eat; yea, come, buy wine and milk without money and without price" (55 : 1).

Redemption is free for all who will have it, Gentile as well as Jew. This is one of the most glorious notes of the gospel. It is particularly moving to discover it in Isaiah as well as in the New Testament.

II. Good Tidings Proclaimed (52 : 1–2,6–7; 54 : 1–8; 55 : 1)

The news the prophet was privileged to proclaim warranted calling out the trumpeters. "Awake, awake" was the rousing cry to a people overcome by dejection and near despair. The time had arrived to be stirred with the hope of new strength and new glory. Jerusalem, figuratively representing the whole nation, was to prepare for a new day. Captive and humbled to the dust, the city was to be clothed in new array and given a renewed mission (52 : 1–2). She was to be characterized by a new knowledge of, and reverence for, the name of her Redeemer and by a new consciousness of his presence and reality.

The marvelous tidings to Israel concerning her re-

demption called forth a hymn of special praise even
for the bearer of the good news (52: 7–8). The prophet
envisioned Jerusalem already reestablished and saw the
approach to Zion of the herald of a new peace and
salvation. The announcement was sounded: "How
beautiful upon the mountains are the feet of him that
bringeth good tidings, that publisheth peace; that
bringeth good tidings of good, that publisheth salvation; that saith unto Zion, Thy God reigneth!"

The city would rise from its desolation with new
hope and unbounded rejoicing as it realized the Lord's
presence at its gates. It was the arrival of him who had
overcome Zion's enemies and had now become her
redeemer. Paul used the words of this prophetic hymn
as an appropriate description of those who preach the
gospel (Rom. 10: 15).

The watchmen who were called upon to lift up their
voices in joy and praise over the coming of the Lord
were said also to "see eye to eye" the return of the
Lord. They saw his coming so directly and positively
that it was as if it were eye to eye. There could be no
mistake either about his coming or his identity. So the
watchmen in strongest tones began to sing in chorus
("together") of his coming and to call the whole city
also to jubilant song (52:9).

The prophet continued to urge Israel to rejoice over
her coming redemption: "Sing, O barren, thou that
didst not bear. . . . Fear not; for thou shalt not be
ashamed. . . . For thy Maker is thine husband; the
Lord of hosts is his name; and thy Redeemer the Holy
One of Israel; The God of the whole earth shall he be
called. For the Lord hath called thee as a woman [wife]
forsaken and grieved in spirit, and a wife of youth,

when thou wast refused, saith thy God" (54:1–6). In this account, the king at the city's gates is seen not as a conqueror or a stranger but as a husband returning to his bride, to "a wife of youth." Tenderly he assured this fallen "wife," "with age-enduring love and kindness I will have compassion and mercy on you. . . . I will not be angry with you or rebuke you. . . . My love and kindness shall not depart from you" (Amplified Version).

What inexpressibly good tidings! What incalculable graciousness and mercy are revealed in these words.

III. Salvation for the "Ends of the Earth" (52:10; 55:4)

The thing which God was about to do for Israel was no provincial matter. The whole earth would witness the event. In the deliverance and redemption of Israel, the nations would see also the strength of the Lord revealed, his "holy arm" made bare. Thus, "the ends of the earth" or the remotest places would be caused to acknowledge him.

The return of the exiles from Babylon would prove to the nations the power of Israel's God to save. Through personal experience, Israel would become a "witness" to this power.

As is true with a number of other passages in Isaiah, there is involved here a larger fulfilment than immediate deliverance of Israel from Chaldean captivity. Luke saw the passage as having its ultimate fulfilment, not in the return of the exiles, but in the birth and ministry of Christ. Referring to this very prophecy, Luke wrote, "All flesh [mankind] shall see the salvation of God" (Luke 3:4–6). As a consequence of the coming and work of Christ, all mankind shall eventually understand and acknowledge the reality of divine redemption as revealed in him.

In a somewhat difficult expression, the same idea as found in Isaiah 52:10 seems to be suggested in 55:4–5. Here it is said, "Behold, I have given him for a witness to the people, a leader and commander to the people. Behold, thou shalt call a nation [nations] that thou knowest not, and nations that knew not thee shall run unto thee because of the Lord thy God, and for the Holy One of Israel; for he hath glorified thee."

Isaiah 55:3, which refers to the "sure mercies of David," could have a historical reference to the mercies specifically given to King David. But it seems best to interpret verses 4 and 5 as referring to a descendant of David, Jesus, the Christ. In any case, Israel is to be a witness to the Gentile nations of God's mercy and salvation. The disciples and apostles, themselves Israelites, were later to preach the gospel to the Gentiles. Through them then, if not before, Israel did bear witness to nations it did not know and also to nations which did not know Israel.

Paul seemed to understand that the promised "sure mercies of David" had actually fallen upon the risen Christ (Acts 13:34). But this does not change the point already made—that through Israel the ends of the earth were to come to know of the salvation which God in his mercy has made available to sinful and fallen mankind.

IV. EVERLASTING COVENANT (55:3,5)

"I will make an everlasting covenant with you" encompasses more than immediate deliverance of Israel.

The covenant concept reached back at least to the days of Abraham, possibly even to Adam and Eve (Gen. 2:16), and forward to the end of time and into eternity. God covenanted with Noah (Gen. 6:18; 9:16), and more than once with Abraham (Gen. 12:1–3; 13:17; 17:2,4,7), and with Israel under Moses (Ex. 19:1–6). Following David's great sin and repentance, God reaffirmed his covenant (2 Sam. 7:8–16), promising that an heir of David would rule forever and that his throne should "be established for ever."

In this passage from Isaiah, the covenant is once more mentioned. To Israel, now chastened, humbled, and dependent, the affirmation of God's eternal faithfulness is underscored and accented.

The covenant always originated with God as his own commitment and assurance of continuing help and unfailing mercy. Though Israel would sin and rebel against God, she would always know that upon her genuine repentance God would have mercy upon her and forgive her. The whole context of this part of the prophecy movingly points up the truth contained in the covenant idea, especially that part which so tenderly portrays God as Israel's husband who still cared for her despite her unfaithfulness.

The continuing hope of a sinful world rests in the fact that God's covenant is an everlasting one. His marvelous salvation is still available to fallen and hopeless humanity.

V. INVITATION UNIVERSALLY EXTENDED (55:1–3a)

It would be difficult to imagine an invitation to salvation more appealing to reason, and at the same time more universally reassuring, than is found in these verses. The thirsty, who are mentioned in verse 1, are assured that waters which satisfy are now available. In a semidesert land like Judah, that promise would take on deeper meaning than we can conceive. "Wine" and "milk," as well as water, were offered. These, too, were scarce, chiefly because water was scarce. Obviously, all three terms are metaphors to designate the spiritual blessings which would strengthen and nourish those who partook of them.

To thirst, to hunger, to labor and never to be satisfied—these ideas graphically describe the condition of men who are outside the will of God. Those who search for something to meet their souls' needs are pictured here as spending money for bread that will not satisfy. The prostration of the masses before idols and false gods now, as then, amounts to no more than this. The modern pathetic and fruitless search for pleasure, power, or position, which can never slake the burning spiritual thirst or gnawing hunger within, is also suggested by the prophet's graphic figure of unsatisfied hunger and unrelieved thirst.

But men need not forever thirst and not be satisfied, or forever be hungry and not be fed. "Hearken diligently unto me," pleads the Lord through the prophet, "and eat ye that which is good, and let your soul delight itself in fatness. Incline your ear, and come unto me: hear, and your soul shall live" (55:2–3).

Only as one eats that which is "good" can his soul truly live. And, as we are aptly reminded, "The true bread and water are the invisible spiritual resources which proceed from God alone." [1] One easily recalls at this point the tragic comment of the Saviour: "And ye will not come to me, that ye might have life."

The prophet's words seem to have been reechoed in the words of Jesus when he spoke of the water of life which a man may drink and thereby find eternal satisfaction and the bread of life which he may eat and never again hunger (John 4:14; 6:51).

VI. FORGIVENESS OFFERED (55:6–9)

Guilt is one of the bedrock problems of human life. Some try vainly to get rid of it by persuading themselves to believe there is no God, and thus no ultimate standard of right and wrong. Others attempt to drown out the voice of conscience by drink, work, or entertainment. Yet the problem does not go away that easily. As Paul Tournier, the eminent Swiss psychiatrist and author, notes in his book *Guilt and Grace,* a vast number of unnecessary illnesses and a large measure of difficulties which lead people needlessly to psychiatrists have their origin in guilt. Assurance of forgiveness is a universal need.

But pardon and forgiveness, in the final analysis, can be obtained only from the one offended. When conscience is sufficiently aroused, it is discovered that the forgiveness which fully satisfies must come from God. Even our sins against ourselves, as well as sins against others, are also offenses against God. One of the golden notes in the gospel proclaimed in Isaiah is that more than forgiveness is available. The wonder is that God actually invites men, and even pleads with them, to come to him for forgiveness.

In 55:6–7 the universal invitation, already expressed in 55:1–2, is reemphasized: "Seek ye the Lord while he may be found, call ye upon him while he is near." But a new element is added here to the earlier invitation. There is the inference that the day of opportunity for pardon may pass, that one can wait too long. This warning was sorely needed by those who loved evil too much to forsake it or could not make up their minds to seek God.

The prophet of the Exile brought a timely warning to the many Jews settled down in Babylon, who were perhaps well-established in business and content with their circumstances. Hesitancy to act or delay in believing what God had promised could be costly. The time had come for repentance. Though the thrilling news that salvation was available had now sounded in their midst, the promised blessings were not unconditional. The people must prepare for them in the only way they could prepare, by a true return in heart to their God.

In the invitation extended here to seek the Lord while opportunity was at hand, the inference is also made, as suggested in the Hebrew text, that they had a right to lay claim upon God for forgiveness. This is well-nigh an audacious thought. It suggests that God's covenant made with the people and his promises given to them placed an obligation upon him to answer if the people would but seek in time. God's honor and integrity are at stake in the promises he has made. This truth constitutes a forceful reason for knowing that if we meet this condition by returning to him and believing on him, we can be sure, as Joel proclaimed and both Peter and Paul affirmed, "Whosoever shall call upon the name of the Lord shall be saved [delivered]." (See Joel 2: 32; Acts 2: 21; Rom. 10:13.)

The way to seek the Lord is made clear in verse 7. The wicked man is to forsake his evil way, the unrighteous man his corrupt thoughts, and "return unto the Lord." Seeking the Lord begins with an awakened conscience and requires one to turn in the Lord's direction. When this turning takes place, the one who turns is cleansed within and gives up his evil practices as well. Too many persons have deluded themselves into thinking that as long as their beliefs are right, it matters little what they do or, for that matter, do not do. But both radical change of conduct and transformation of thought are required. Abundant pardon is certain for those who heed both requirements.

The phrase "abundantly pardon" is literally "multiply to pardon" or "he will be great to pardon." More is involved than merely obtaining mercy. It implies the continual discovery of more and more of his gracious favor. Jesus assured us that his purpose in coming was to provide life and life "more abundantly" (John 10: 10). The abundant life comes only to those who hear the gracious invitation and turn to the Lord for this great pardoning mercy.

VII. The Word for the World (55:10-13)

Verse 1 of this chapter, as we have already seen, sounds a universal invitation. Verses 10–13 signify the certain world-wide proclamation of God's word.

It has been pointed out that verse 10 includes almost every element of such agricultural parables of Jesus as that of the sower (Matt. 13: 18–43). That parable also deals with various responses given by men to the Word of God.

As universal as moisture, provided the earth in the form of rain or snow, will be the spread of his Word around the world. That Word may be presumed from the content to be about salvation. In terms of the thought of Isaiah, as is true of the New Testament, that Word is the good news (gospel) of God's redeeming love and purpose.

God's Word, like the mysterious powers of germination in nature, will be effective also in all the world. Nor will it return unto him fruitless when rightly proclaimed. Its consequence in, and its impact upon, human life will be miraculous. Peace and joy will be produced by it. Mountains and hills will ring with song because of it. Even the trees will "clap their hands" as a result of it (vv. 11–12).

Using such masterful metaphors as the above, the prophet predicted the transforming power of the good news of salvation. The change in men would be as if fir trees came up instead of thorns and myrtle trees instead of briers (v. 13). Thus, the prophet gave expression to the glorious and universal efficacy of the Word. God's Word will be as a name of identification, a memorial by which he will be known in all the earth.

To Israel, shortly to go out from captivity, this word of salvation would become precious as a name of renown and an everlasting sign. Its meaning has been found no less precious to every other soul who has come truly to understand the good news of God's redeeming power.

---

[1] *The Interpreter's Bible, op. cit.*, p. 644.

9

GOD'S THREE R'S

As EDUCATION, according to the old adage, consists basically of the three R's of "reading, 'riting, and 'rithmetic," true religion, in the view of Isaiah, rests upon three R's also: righteousness, repentance toward God, and redemption.

I. RIGHTEOUSNESS (56:1-2; 58:1-14; 59:2-18)

Old Testament prophets were noted for resounding and repeated emphasis on justice and righteous living. Understanding of God's unceasing and uncompromising expectation of truth, integrity, moral purity, and justice was distinctive of all these "holy men of old" and certainly of Isaiah. Accent in the pulpit upon such themes as he stressed is still called prophetic preaching. The test of any religion or religious profession is its ethical and moral standards. Beliefs are important; but they are only superficial, or worse, unless life is changed by them.

1. *Unrighteousness Noted*

Isaiah 56, 57, and 58 are given chiefly to ethical instructions. Chapter 56 begins, "Thus saith the Lord, Keep ye judgment, and do justice." This is a call for both justice and righteousness. Those who heed the call are said to be blessed.

The particular concerns pointed out in 56:2 are observance of the sabbath and keeping one's "hand" from doing evil. Though the statement is brief, the implications are vast: Those who please God must keep the law both as it relates to reverence toward God and to purity of personal life.

In 58:1–14, the same truth is pointed out even more impressively. The chapter begins: "Cry aloud, spare not, lift up thy voice like a trumpet, and shew my people their transgression." In the loudest voice, as with the awakening thunder of a trumpet, Israel was warned of the deep moral failures of the nation. Paradoxically, when the people apparently objected to the charge, the Lord acknowledged that formal practice of worship actually had not ceased. Indeed, God said through the prophet: "They seek me daily, and delight to know my ways, as a nation that did righteousness, and forsook not the ordinance of their God." Ostensibly the people were ever so devout. Perhaps they added that they even took delight in "approaching to God" (literally, the nearness of God). Religious services were popular and possibly well-attended. But the people had got little good out of them. This was evident from their complaint, "Wherefore have we fasted, . . . and thou seest not?" Their services were really without meaning. The reason is not hard to discover: "Behold, O Israel, in the day of your fast [when you should be grieving for your sins] you find business profit, and [instead of stopping all work, as the Law implies you and your workmen should] you extort from your hired servants a full amount of labor" (58:3, Amplified).

God was not pleased with the kind of worship which

consisted only of piously bowing the head in public fasts when there was no relationship between this act and daily life. Not even clothing of sackcloth and ashes could hide improper attitudes and purposes of the heart. "Wilt thou call this a fast," asked the Lord through the prophet in burning satire, "and an acceptable day to the Lord?"

2. God's Standard of Righteousness

In great contrast to the kind of empty fasting being practiced, God set forth his standard: "Is not this the fast that I have chosen? to loose the bands of wickedness, to undo the heavy burdens, and to let the oppressed go free, and that ye break every yoke?" (58:6). The people had not really been concerned to worship God. Even in their very acts of devotion, their thoughts were only on how they could take advantage of others and how they could press for personal gain. In their fast days, they were not seeking God's pleasure but their own (v. 3). Their minds were occupied only with their business affairs, not their spiritual needs. Though they oppressed their workers and took advantage of the poor on every hand, they thought their acts of piety could satisfy God!

True righteousness required that the people "loose the bands of wickedness," undo heavy burdens placed upon the poor, give freedom to the oppressed, and break every yoke placed upon other necks. Maintaining right personal relationships and accepting responsibility for the less fortunate were required. As long as the people sought their own pleasure instead of God's, it did not matter how frequent their formal religious rites might be. "Is it not to deal thy bread to the hungry, and that thou bring the poor that are cast out to thy house? when thou seest the naked, that thou cover him; and that thou hide not thyself from thine own flesh?" (v. 7).

One may well wonder if there is an echo of this prophecy in Christ's description of those on the left in the judgment scene of Matthew 25:31–46.

The emphasis in verse 6 is on social compassion and liberation of the poor. Every yoke of human bondage for which the people were responsible was to be broken. Honest solicitude for human welfare and liberty was to possess their hearts. The hungry, the oppressed, the homeless, the debtors, and the slaves were to be recognized as the proper concern of those who would "delight to draw near to God" (RSV).

Some of the sufferers who were being neglected were, strangely enough, relatives of those who pretended to be righteous. Paul was aware of God's high standards when he wrote, "[God] hath made of one blood all nations . . . of the earth" (Acts 17:26). Does his comment actually enlarge the compass of Christian responsibility to include all peoples and races? In a day when masses are starving and oppressed, this is an awesome thought.

3. *The Rewards of Righteousness*

Glorious promises and assurances were given those who would respond to God's directions: "Then shall thy light break forth as the morning, and thine health shall spring forth speedily."

The phrase, "and thy righteousness shall go before thee," suggests that even in the eyes of the world Israel's fear of the Lord would be recognized. The prophet also added, "The glory of the Lord shall be thy rereward [rear guard]." Best of all, if they would put things right with their fellowmen and would truly seek the pleasure of the Lord rather than their own, they were assured, "Then shalt thou call, and the Lord shall answer" (v. 9).

The mystery of why God does not answer our prayers for revival may have at least one of its explanations in this passage. Israel was to understand that, despite fasting and religious rites and supposed seeking of the Lord and multiplying of fasts, they could have no answer unless they heeded the laws of justice and righteousness. If they conformed to God's will, they would have great spiritual refreshing. He would answer. Indeed, he would tenderly respond, as a mother to the distressed call of a child, saying, "Here I am!" He would be in their very midst to help and to save. But the people must remove unjust yokes and cease "the putting forth of the finger, and speaking vanity" (v. 9).

The phrase "the putting forth of the finger" likely means an attitude of contempt. "Speaking vanity" means "speaking wickedness" (RSV).

Righteousness requires that men's souls be drawn toward the hungry, their desire being to satisfy the afflicted. Such compassion could result in the turning of midnight darkness into noonday (v. 10). It would also satisfy the soul's drought and make the people "like a watered garden, and like a spring of water, whose waters fail not" (v. 11).

If men would meet the Lord's conditions of righteous conduct, proper observance of the sabbath, and concern for others, "not doing thine own ways, nor finding thine own pleasure, nor speaking thine own words: Then shalt thou delight thyself in the Lord." They would also be exalted and honored and made to "ride upon the high places of the earth." Theirs would be a victorious march, filled with enjoyment of all the heritage promised them as God's people (v. 14).

Some think most of Isaiah 56–66, especially the present passage, was written after Israel's restoration to Palestine. This opinion is based upon mention here of the sabbath and such temple observances as fasting. Others feel that such a conclusion is doubtful and that an earlier date is indicated. Whatever the time of the prophecy, the message is meaningful: that God's promises made in this passage are conditional. This point is emphasized even by the repeated "ifs" found in the chapter. (See vv. 9–10, 13.)

God's conditions for fulfilment of his promises can never be met by mere observance of religious rites. As important as true worship is, not even this can be a substitute for justice, compassion, service toward others, genuine devotion to the Lord, and humble trust in him (Matt. 23:23). Those who observe these requirements will become as a watered garden in a desert land.

II. Repentance (57:6–21; 59:13–16)

Israel's failure to attain the spiritual influence and usefulness suggested in 58:11–14 was not because of God's inability to save or his inattention to the people's plea. The Lord's hand was not shortened that it could not save, or his ear dulled that it could not hear. The reason for Israel's lack of spiritual power is clearly stated: "But your iniquities have separated between you and your God, and your sins have hid his face from you, that he will not hear" (59:2).

1. *Cause for Repentance*

What were these sins of which Israel needed to repent? To be specific in an explanation of the grievances discussed in these verses would require one to be specific about the date of writing. However, the list of sins for which Israel needed to repent could be dated pre-exilic, exilic, or postexilic. Israel did not seem to learn from past failures. Sadly, though, these same verses could describe the sins of many of the world's people in 1969. The prophet declared that the hands of the people were defiled with the blood of those they had wronged, their fingers with evildoings. No one sought to deal justly within the courts but to gain special advantage. The charge, "no one goes to law honestly," (RSV) has a familiar ring. The words, "Your lips have spoken lies," reveal a tragic decay of integrity. Deeds of violence were also perpetrated (v. 6b). Rather than being swift to do good, their feet were quick to run to evil. Their thoughts dwelt not on purity and ways to please God, but on iniquity. There is a modern sound to another charge against Israel: "Desolation and destruction are in their highways" (RSV).

Not only was Israel not seeking every possible way to peace, but wickedness and perverseness were in all of her actions. Moral decline, carelessness about social responsibility, and indifference to justice had become a way of life. Note that up to this point the prophet has used the third person in his indictments—*they*. Then, in verse 12, the prophet spoke on behalf of the people and confessed their sin. "Therefore justice is far from us, and righteousness does not overtake us; we look for light, and behold, darkness, and for brightness, but we walk in gloom" (v. 9, RSV). The nation groped as the blind for its way and stumbled as in the night. And all of this even at the noontide of God's intended purpose for her! (v. 10). The reason is repeated: "For our transgressions are multiplied before thee, and our sins testify against us" (v. 12, RSV).

Justice was turned back and righteousness stood afar off. Truth was strangely absent in the streets, the courts, the public square, and the marketplace. Obviously, repentance was the only solution.

The verb in the phrase, "Yea, truth faileth" (v. 15), could be translated "is banished" or "is missing." It indicates that truth was considered nonessential or even folly. No wonder the Lord saw this and it displeased him! The understatement thunders with significance. Such conduct could only deserve judgment (v. 18).

The promises given Israel were great and marvelous. The hope of salvation, so brilliantly set forth by the prophet, was at the threshold of realization. But that realization depended upon genuine confession of sin and repentance.

In chapter 57, a vivid and forceful complaint had been registered against Israel for continuing to turn to idols. She was asked by the Lord, "Should I receive comfort [shall I be appeased for] in these [things]?" (57:6). The people had also exhausted their strength climbing mountains to worship at the shrines of heathen gods (57:7–8), deceiving themselves all the while (57:10). However, only those who would take refuge in God could actually inherit his holy mountain (57:13). God dwells not only in the high and holy place, it was proclaimed, but also in the contrite and humble spirit (57:15). Only against those who keep on backsliding must his wrath be continued (57:17).

2. *Recognition of Need for Repentance*

An essential step toward genuine repentance is an honest recognition of need. The prodigal would perhaps never have returned had he not "come to himself." The prophet saw not only the agony caused by the sins of the people, but honestly confessed these sins before God. "For our transgressions," he said, placing himself among the people, "are multiplied before thee, and our sins testify against us: for our transgressions are with us; and as for our iniquities, we know them" (59:12). Genuine sincerity would compel the people to acknowledge the continued multiplication of their wrongs. These very wrongs, in truth, bore witness against them. They fairly wreaked with the offenses of their sin. The people needed to acknowledge the sins as "our iniquities," not to make excuses for them. More than that, they needed to confess that "we know them."

There are sins which men wish to ignore but cannot; which they want to deny but must not; which they try to blame on others but, if honest, will not. Conscience finally demands that the guilty admit "we know them." Though such honesty is painful, it offers promise of one's seeking forgiveness and forsaking his iniquities.

3. *Hope for the Penitent*

The penitent can be comforted in the knowledge that God will heal, lead, and restore. Israel had been persistent in her backsliding, thus causing God to hide his face. But his unceasing desire was to forgive and to restore. The remark "and restore comforts unto him and to his mourners" was apparently a reinforced assurance of this; and the phrase "his mourners" a reference to those who repent in deep contrition.

For all who repent there would come such fulness of joy that the "fruit of the lips," perhaps meaning the "praise of the lips," will be, "Peace, peace to him that is far off, and to him that is near" (57: 19).

In the New Testament, we are told of Christ who himself is our peace and who "came and preached peace to you who were far off and peace to those who were near" (Eph. 2: 17, RSV). The apostle understood both Jew and Gentile to be included, the "near" being the former and those "afar off" the latter. But even in the days of the prophet, it was proclaimed that there can be no peace for the wicked (57: 21). To those who persist in evil, the future was and is "like the troubled sea, when it cannot rest, whose waters cast up mire and dirt" (57: 20).

This poetic portrayal of a morally corrupt society all too vividly suggests the present condition of our society. What mire and dirt the troubled waters are presently washing across the shores of our land! Surely the conditions producing these angry seas, loaded as they are with the nauseous by-products of human iniquity, are as much a cause for offense toward God now as they were then.

4. *Alternative to Repentance*

The hope of Israel was to acknowledge her apostate deeds and, in penitence, to turn from them. Divine judgment against the sins enumerated in 59: 13–15 could no longer be restrained. God must act! Seeing that no man stood at his side in pursuit of justice (v. 16), God would gird himself for the purging and chastening which were essential (v. 17). His clothing would be the breastplate of righteousness, the helmet of salvation, the garments of vengeance. He would require men to repay according to their deed. Retributive judgment would fall on both Israel and the nations at large. Much of the same armor with which the Lord is said here to clothe himself is mentioned by Paul as garments with which the Christian should cover himself in his conflict with the rulers of the darkness of this world (Eph. 6: 11–17).

Judgment was Israel's alternative to repentance. God's justice is no less a reality than his love. Love without justice would be a contradiction, as justice without mercy would be a travesty. The Scriptures declare that "God is love" (1 John 4: 16). They declare also that "our God is a consuming fire" (Heb. 12: 29).

III. REDEMPTION (59: 20–21)

God never wants his chastening to be an end in itself. Only man's persistence in sin makes it so. God desires that men respond to the influences of his mercy. He causes the rain to fall upon both the just and the unjust alike. But if his goodness does not turn men to repentance, judgment becomes essential.

1. *Redemptive Purposes*

God's ultimate goal is redemptive. This the prophet continued to declare: "So shall they fear the name of the Lord from the west, and his glory from the rising of the sun" (59: 19).

When Israel was caused by her chastening to turn to the Lord, she was the beneficiary of his gracious mercy and protecting care. The nations were to be moved by her experience also to fear the Lord (v. 19).

More was foreseen than physical deliverance of Israel. Spiritual redemption would ensue: "And the Redeemer shall come to Zion, and unto them that turn from transgression in Jacob, saith the Lord" (v. 20). The nation again would become the channel of his covenant purpose and spiritual blessings would flow through her across the centuries and forever (v. 21).

The above promise seems to have looked distinctly beyond even the restoration of Jerusalem. The coming of the Redeemer to his people would mean not only salvation but glorious fulfilment. Paul understood this promise to have its highest culmination in the redemptive work of Christ. He saw both Israel and the Gentiles as included in the promise. Referring to this passage in Isaiah, he wrote, "So all Israel shall be saved: as it is written, There shall come out of Sion the Deliverer, and shall turn away ungodliness from Jacob: For this is my covenant unto them, when I shall take away their sins" (Rom. 11:26–27).

2. *Need for Redemption*

The physical restoration of Jerusalem was included in the prophet's prediction. But this was only a part of what was to come to pass. Spiritual regeneration was the larger goal. Indeed, the context makes clear that the latter would be a condition for realization of the former. There must be spiritual return to the Lord for light to break at all in that darkened city of ruins. If Israel would turn from her transgressions, God would come in his mercy to redeem. In the whole of chapter 59, the movement is toward this grand climax.

The sins of the people were cataloged as lies, the shedding of innocent blood, wickedness, wasting and destruction, denying the Lord, injustice. These all revealed how greatly the people needed salvation. Only the Redeemer could deliver them from the webs of sin in which they had clothed themselves (59:6). The separation between God and the people, caused alone by sin, had been deep, tragic, and costly. Israel had broken the covenant which God had made with her. But God had not forgotten his covenant.

Filled with painful dread and fear, roaring like bears in trouble and moaning like doves in anxiety, the people had wondered when justice would come. They looked for salvation but thought it "far off from us" (59:11). Their lament over their wretched condition was known, however, to the Lord. God saw that there was no human power available to intervene and to save (v. 16); no arm besides his mighty enough to deliver. The armor with which he would clothe himself would be not only for judgment but also for salvation (vv. 17–18).

3. *Ultimate Redemption*

Consequences of God's redemption for Israel and for the world are impressively set forth in chapter 60. The closing line of chapter 59 reveals that the words God had put in their mouth would not depart from Israel or from her children's children. Then, in 60:1 the people are called upon to fulfil their glorious purpose: "Arise, shine; for thy light is come."

The coming Servant of the Lord depicted in 61:1–3

would preach good tidings (the gospel) to the meek,
bind up the brokenhearted, proclaim liberty to the
captives, free the imprisoned, announce the acceptable
year of the Lord and the day of vengeance of God,
and comfort all that mourn. That this prophecy had
both physical and spiritual dimensions seems obvious.
God, as the Redeemer of Israel, would set the captives
free, open their prison doors, proclaim good tidings to
the meek and the acceptable year of the Lord. He
would also comfort those that mourned, give them
beauty for ashes, a garment of praise for the spirit of
heaviness. All this he would do that he might be glorified in the redemptive work he had wrought.

The above prediction had a historical fulfilment in
Israel's return from exile and in her spiritual influence
since. But the prediction evidently reached beyond
this fulfilment. Its greatest realization was to be in the
work of the Messiah.

In Isaiah the term Redeemer is used at least thirteen
times, more than in any other book in the Bible. Only
four other usages of the term are found elsewhere. The
prophet referred to the Lord both as "thy Redeemer,
the Holy One of Israel," and "our Redeemer—the Lord
of hosts" (RSV). He quoted the Lord himself as saying, "You shall know that I, the Lord, am your Savior
and your Redeemer, the Mighty One of Jacob"
(60:16, RSV).

Following the resurrection, two men were on their
way to Emmaus when Jesus joined them. The men,
taking him to be a stranger, confessed concerning the
one who had been crucified: "But we trusted that it
had been he which should have redeemed Israel" (Luke
24:21). Later, Paul wrote, "But when the fulness of

the time was come, God sent forth his Son, made of a woman, made under the law, To redeem them that were under the law, that we might receive the adoption of sons" (Gal. 4: 4–5).

In Jesus, it would then appear, the prophetic promise in Isaiah reached its consummation. In the New Testament view, the Servant of Jehovah and the Messiah are one and the same person. The words of Isaiah 61: 1–3 describe perfectly the mission of the Messiah. And in Luke 4: 18–19 Jesus became his own interpreter. Matthew Henry puts the matter succinctly: "He that is the best expositor of Scripture gives us the best exposition of these words. He declared they were fulfilled in himself." This passage, therefore, as another has well said, "is not for an age but for all time." In it the essence of the gospel, the glad tidings of God's redemption, is set forth in immortal terms.

10

FOR ALL THE WORLD

Two colossal ideas are brought together, perhaps distinctively so, in the prophecy of Isaiah:

1. The vicarious suffering of the Servant of the Lord for the redemption of man.
2. The inclusion of all the world in God's redemptive purpose.

The first of these was examined in the chapter on Isaiah 52:13 to 53:12. The second now calls for consideration.

Isaiah proclaimed that all nations are included in God's love and redemptive plan. For this reason, the people of God are destined in God's purpose to be witnesses to all nations. Through this witness all peoples eventually will come to know the salvation of the Lord.

Isaiah saw God's rule as the "hand that is stretched out over all the nations" (14:26, RSV). He declared, "The Lord has bared his holy arm before the eyes of all the nations; and all the ends of the earth shall see the salvation of our God" (52:10, RSV). He further said, "For as the earth brings forth its shoots, and as a garden causes what is sown in it to spring up, so the Lord God will cause righteousness and praise to spring forth before all the nations" (61:11, RSV). And again, "He shall judge between the nations, and shall decide for many peoples; and they shall beat their swords into plowshares, and their spears into pruning hooks; nation shall not lift up sword against nation, neither shall they learn war any more" (2:4, RSV). All nations are called upon to recognize the displeasure of the Lord against evil (34:1–2). The vicarious work of the Suffering Servant would be for all nations (52:15). Israel would be used to call nations whom they had not known and nations which had not known them to knowledge of the Lord (55:5). The day would come when the "root of Jesse" should stand as an ensign to the Gentiles and "to it shall the Gentiles [nations] seek" (11:10). The Servant of God would bring forth justice to the nations (42:1) and light to those who sit in darkness (42:6–7).

Thus, in many and varied ways the prophet was led to speak of God's sovereignty over all the nations and of his unceasing concern for them.

I. A Glorious Ingathering (56:6–8; 60:3–7)

The phrase in 56:7, "For mine house shall be called an house of prayer for all people," has been made familiar to New Testament readers by Jesus' own use of it (Matt. 21:13; Luke 19:46). This phrase is found in a context which refers to the wall of separation that had been erected by the Jews between themselves and the eunuchs and proselytes. That wall would be removed. Neither stranger nor eunuch thereafter would have to say, "Behold, I am a dry tree." A dry tree refers to a useless or barren one. Hereafter, both strangers and eunuchs would have an honorable place in the service and worship of the Lord and should be accepted on equal terms. God's house would thus be open to them as fully as to others. The eunuchs had, perhaps through no fault of their own, been doomed to have no children to perpetuate their names. To them also would be given an "everlasting name which shall not be cut off" (RSV). Moreover, "Even them will I bring to my holy mountain, and make them joyful in my house of prayer" (v. 7). Here one is reminded of the Ethiopian eunuch whom Philip led to Christ.

The worship of God in the New Age will know no exclusivism or barriers. His house will be called the house of prayer "for all people." The place of worship will be primarily for communion with him, thus "an house of prayer." A religion acceptable to the Lord is one which is concerned for and brings together all nations. God, who had gathered the outcasts of Israel, now declared "Yet will I gather others . . . beside those that are gathered" (v. 8).

Foreigners, as well as the outcasts of Israel, are to be brought to God's holy mountain. The universality of his redemptive purpose and the availability of his salvation to everyone are thus underscored. Through the prophet God declared what Jesus would later make more explicit: "Other sheep I have, which are not of this fold: them also I must bring, and they shall hear my voice; and there shall be one fold, and one shepherd" (John 10: 16).

When repentant and restored Israel fulfils its mission, "the Gentiles [nations] shall come to thy light, and kings to the brightness of thy rising." Zion, now redeemed, will become a light to all the nations. Among the multitudes who will be drawn to Zion will also be her own scattered sons and daughters (v. 4).

That this prophecy carried hope for the Jew of the restored glory and influence of Jerusalem is perhaps unquestioned. But it carried overtones of vastly greater significance. One scholar points out that the prophet foresaw not only the future restoration of Jerusalem as a place of exaltation and worldly success, but he also saw "blended together every thing that is in the future to produce this glory, from the first weak beginnings till the consummation in the heavenly Jerusalem. . . . It is obvious that here again the Prophet draws the picture of the future with the colors of the present." [1]

All who gather from the many nations will show forth the praises of the Lord (60:3-6). "And I," said the Lord, "will glorify the house of my glory" (60:7). And this he will do by drawing all mankind to his glorious house. One respected expositor, Delitzsch, wrote that God will make his house's inward glory like the outward, adorning it with the gifts presented by the converted Gentile world.

Some think the picture painted by the prophet encompasses what is spoken of in Revelation as the New Jerusalem coming down from God out of heaven (Rev. 21:2-10; 22:2-7). The important point, however, is that God's redemptive purpose set forth in the prophecy envisions the gathering into one of a great fellowship of peoples from all the nations. And in that fellowship God himself will be glorified.

II. A NEW HEAVEN AND A NEW EARTH (65:17-25)

By any reasonable standard of interpretation, the portrait painted in this passage is unforgettable. It is etched with the delicacy and beauty of a masterpiece. Even those who see in it only the poetic vision of a new

age for the city of Jerusalem, built on the sad and deso-
late ruins of its past, agree it reveals a future radiant
with hope. The new day will be marked with peace,
prosperity, and goodwill beyond anything previously
known. For those who see this prophecy as reaching
beyond the history of natural Jerusalem, the portrait
takes on even greater significance. It suggests a golden
future beyond anything history has as yet recorded.

The prophet had previously unfolded the mighty
changes which would occur both as a consequence of
the judgment of God upon evil and the grace of God
given in redemption. At this point in the prophecy, he
depicted the coming of new heavens and a new earth
as God's special creation (v. 17a). So great and marvelous will this new creation be that it will erase from
memory the agonies and sorrows of the old (v. 17b).

The phrase "new heavens and a new earth" possibly
means a new universe or cosmos. The language in
2 Peter 3 : 13 indicates that in New Testament days the
fulfilment of this prophecy was considered to lie in
the future: "Nevertheless we, according to his promise,
look for new heavens and a new earth, wherein
dwelleth righteousness." The writer of Revelation also
looked for the coming of a new heaven and new earth:
"And I saw a new heaven and a new earth: for the first
heaven and the first earth were passed away; and there
was no more sea" (21 : 1).

Those who inhabit the new heaven and earth have
reason to be glad and rejoice forever. God will make
Jerusalem, either typifying this new heaven and earth
or else situated in it, a rejoicing and her people a joy
(v. 18). The voice of weeping and of crying, so often
heard in the old city, will be heard no more (v. 19).

The vitality of its citizens will not be diminished by the passing of the years (v. 20). Men will be able to enjoy the fruits of their labors undeterred by fear of death or trouble (vv. 21–23). Moreover, they are assured, "Before they call, I will answer."

As a reminder of the rebellion and sinfulness of Israel in the past, chapter 65 begins, "I was ready to be sought by those who did not ask for me. I said, 'Here am I, here am I,' to a nation that did not call on my name" (RSV). Israel had also been reminded that when God had thus offered to answer, the incredible reply he had received was, " 'Keep to yourself, do not come near me, for I am set apart from you' " (65:5, RSV). There had been times though, when suffering great anguish and conscious of grave need, the people had cried out, "O that thou wouldst rend the heavens and come down, that the mountains might quake at thy presence" (64:1, RSV). But in this new heaven and earth, God will answer even before the people call. He will anticipate their need; and, while they are yet speaking, he will pour out his blessing upon them (v. 24).

Such peace and tranquility will mark this new creation of God that the wolf and the lamb will feed together, the lion will eat straw like a domesticated bullock, and the serpent, instead of bruising the heels of men, will feed upon the dust of the earth. God assures that nothing will hurt or destroy in all his holy mountain (v. 25).

It should be remembered that the above prophecy is expressed in poetic imagery. To press each word and phrase for a literal meaning would not be in keeping with the nature of the writing. The essential message of the passage is that a day will come when God's work in the struggle with evil and with all that has wreaked devastation on mankind will be consummated. This is a glorious part of the good tidings Isaiah so masterfully set forth. And it is the promise inherent in the gospel of Jesus Christ.

III. ALL NATIONS TO SEE HIS GLORY (66:18–24)

This passage chiefly proclaims that God will eventually reveal his glory to all nations. He who knows men's works and even their thoughts will come and gather all nations and tongues to himself (v. 18). They will then behold and perceive the glory of him who is Lord of all.

God will set a sign among the nations, those afar as well as those that are near. People who have not heard of his fame or glory will be won to him and, consequently, will declare the glory of God among the nations (v. 19). Ultimately they are to bring their brethren like an offering unto the Lord out of all nations, even the distant ones (vv. 19–20). The various means of transportation by which the prophet envisioned men coming to Zion suggest the response of all kinds and classes of people. The haste with which they come suggests their great desire to know and worship God. It is striking to note that some of those brought out of Gentile nations will be made priests and Levites unto the Lord (v. 21). This may refer to the Gentile or non-Jewish followers of the Messiah who are ultimately to help bear the gospel to all parts of the earth.

The new heaven and new earth promised in 65:17 will be enduring (v. 22). It will remain "before me" said the Lord. "So shall your seed and your name remain," he added. Worship before him will continue regularly and faithfully: "And it shall come to pass, that from one new moon to another, and from one sabbath to another, shall all flesh come to worship before me, saith the Lord" (v. 23). This worship, it is said, will be *before* him, not necessarily in the Temple. Could this refer to the congregations all over the earth which gather locally in his presence for worship? Some think it may even point beyond this, as does the book of Revelation, to the eternal blessedness of the redeemed.

Verses 22 and 23 provide a grand climax. "God's people, like the new creation, will endure forever [Jer. 31:34–36] and a mighty chorus of praises will ceaselessly rise to God's throne" (The Oxford Annotated Bible).

In contrast with the above, a solemn note must now be sounded: The vision of the redeemed, gathered from all the earth and beholding his glory without ceasing, cannot be ended without the final grave reminder of that which awaits the wicked and all who refuse the redemption God gloriously offers. The awesomeness of this scene has caused many to wish the book had ended with verse 22. But for it to have done so would have been to leave the reader without a grave and needed revelation. That revelation is that both the glory and the inescapable consequence of human freedom require personal choice. And that choice has destiny in it.

Judgment and justice, however harsh they may seem against the backdrop of the inspiring portrayal of a new heaven and new earth, are also an essential part of the gospel. If there were no ultimate judgment and no justice, the good news of God's salvation would be meaningless. Still worse, it would become evident that there is really no God through whose mercy man may find redemption. Logic appears to demand that if there be a God at all, he be both a God of love and a God of justice.

If the judgment predicted by the prophet seems too severe, it will be remembered that our Lord himself used some of the very thought expressed here when he spoke of those who would go into torment "where their worm dieth not, and the fire is not quenched" (Mark 9:44). The prophet cannot be faithful unless he proclaims both aspects of God's nature, his love and his justice. He must preach the blessedness of accepting redemption and the tragedy of rejecting it.

Though the last words of the prophecy are a warning, the dominant note of Isaiah, especially in chapters 40–66, concerns the good tidings of God's gracious mercy and eternal salvation. This is the grandeur of the book; this is the Gospel in Isaiah.

IV. CONCLUSION

And how unutterably needful, even amidst the triumphs of this so-called space age, is that gospel.

That Isaiah speaks relevantly and with reassuring power to our day, as it has to others, is undeniable. Obviously, the prophecy contains strong and repeated warnings of judgment upon sin—the sins of injustice, moral corruption, disregard of truth, unconcern for the poor and oppressed, and hypocrisy in religion. But, happily, Isaiah is not distinctive for its warning about judgment. Its greater message is that the God of justice and Lord of the universe is also a compassionate and merciful Father. His justice is not merely tempered by his mercy. It is only the other side of the coin. His grace is greater than human need is deep. His marvelous grace is greater than all our sin.

More brilliantly disclosed in chapters 40 to 66, but reappearing throughout the prophecy, is God's desire and intention to save his people. This fact breaks forth again and again with the brilliance of the noonday sun. No other book of the Old Testament more fully discloses God's plan to deliver his people. The Jews supposed this deliverance related only to the Exile. But the New Testament affirms that what God intended had dimensions of greater depth. It included, if indeed it did not primarily concern, all that Christ, the Word made flesh, declared he came into the world to accomplish. Isaiah more than suggests the marvelous *good news* the New Testament enunciates. It foretokens it.

How this world needs such *good news*! "Wherever we look," comments an editorial in one of the nation's most popular weekly magazines, "something's wrong."

Crises—military, monetary, social, governmental, moral—stagger the mind. Crime in America has increased 88 percent in the past decade, while population rose only 6 percent. A major crime was reported to have been committed every eight seconds in 1967 and the record still grows worse. America is reaching "the limits of the power of its institutions and convictions," charges a German observer.

Church attendance is declining; membership, though high, has leveled off. The uncertain trumpets, sounded by radical elements within, more than attacks of enemies from without, have left church members confused, church leaders often confounded, and the non-Christian world comfortable in its sins or, worse, caught up in its despair.

Headline attention is given a strange breed of so-called radical theologians (theologians who of all men are supposed to have some dependable word about God). Some even call themselves "Christian atheists" and report that God is dead. Certain prominent church-men deny historic validity to the faith of our fathers. A creeping paralysis of institutionalized self-centeredness among church members tends to displace self-giving service to the whole world. In a day like this, the good news that God's eternal purpose to redeem man—at least a remnant who repent and seek his way—deserves the inspired pen of an Isaiah.

The book of Isaiah came out of a world not essentially unlike our own. Though details differed, human nature and the human plight were much the same as now. Actually, in most of the centuries of man's existence the ceiling of hope has often hung exceedingly low. Except where a ray of divine sunlight has broken through and the clouds have been swept away by the mercy of God, there has been no hope.

Isaiah is rooted deeply in reality. There was no glossing over the agony, hopelessness, cynicism, political intrigue, religious emptiness, and self-deception of the era in which the prophecy was born. But the winds of God's mercy were rising. Through rifts they made in the lowering skies, the prophet saw the sunlight of divine assurance and salvation. With inspiration born out of remarkable vision of the glory and purpose of God, he set down the eternally good news we have found in the book. That news guarantees that there still is hope! God intends to move on toward the fulfilment of his ancient covenant! The repentant may be sure not only that God *can* but *will* save.

For Baptists, on the eve of the great Crusade of the Americas, the book of Isaiah cannot but have special meaning. Their confidence that the good news in Isaiah and the subsequent gospel of the New Testament, which it foreshadowed, affords unfailing hope of man's deliverance even in our day enables them to expect, even as they pray for, a mighty spiritual awakening. It inspires the hope that multitudes now bound in a kind of modern exile may see the salvation of God.

Hearing God's continuing call, "Whom shall I send, and who will go for us?" may every Christian respond: "Here am I; send me." Heaven's glorious invitation, "Come now, and let us reason together, saith the Lord: though your sins be as scarlet, they shall be as white as snow; though they be red like crimson, they shall be as wool," never needed more to be heard.

---

[1] John Peter Lange, *Commentary on the Holy Scriptures* (Grand Rapids: Zondervan Publishing House, 1960), VI, 647.

Suggested Audiovisual Materials

A filmstrip (50 frames, color, recording) has been prepared specifically for use in connection with the study of THE GOSPEL IN ISAIAH. It will be effective to show this filmstrip at some time prior to the first class period. Produced by Broadman Films, *The Gospel in Isaiah* is available from your Baptist Book Store.

Other projected aids will prove valuable as extracurricular materials. Selected frames may be used as interest centers.

Filmstrips:

> *The Gospel in Isaiah,* 50 frames, color, recording
> *A Demand for Holiness—Isaiah,* 30 frames, color
> *Isaiah,* 36 frames, color
> *Isaiah, Statesman for God,* 59 frames, color, recording
> *Prophet-poet of the Exile,* 46 frames, color, recording
> *Vision of Isaiah,* 49 frames, color, recording

Bibliography *

Allis, Oswald Thompson. *Unity of Isaiah*. Nutley, New Jersey: Presbyterian & Reformed Publishing Company, 1950.

Black, M., and Rowley, H. H. *Peake's Commentary on the Bible*. Camden, New Jersey: Nelson-National, 1962.

Blackwood, Andrew. *Preaching from the Prophetic Books*. Nashville, Tennessee: Abingdon Press, 1951.

Blank, Seldon. *The Prophetic Faith in Isaiah*. New York: Harper & Row, 1950.

Buttrick, George A., ed. *The Interpreter's Bible*, V. New York: Abingdon Press, 1957.

Driver, S. R. *Isaiah, His Life and Times*. Westwood, New Jersey: Fleming H. Revell Company, n.d.

Eason, J. Lawrence. *New Bible Survey*. Grand Rapids: Zondervan Publishing House, 1963.

Davidson, Stibbs, and Kevan. *The New Bible Commentary*. Grand Rapids: William B. Eerdmans Publishing Company, 1953.

Francisco, Clyde T. *Introducing the Old Testament*. Nashville: Broadman Press, 1950.

Harrelson, Walter. *Interpreting the Old Testament*. New York: Holt, Rinehart, and Winston, 1964.

Jennings, F. C. *Isaiah*. Neptune, New Jersey: Loizeaux Brothers, Incorporated, 1966.

Keil, Carl F., and Delitzsch, Franz. *Commentaries on the Old Testament*. Volumes 1 & 2, Grand Rapids: William B. Eerdmans Publishing Company, 1960.

Lange, John Peter. *Commentary on the Holy Scriptures*. Grand Rapids: Zondervan Publishing House, 1960.

Leslie, Elmer A. *Isaiah*. Nashville: Abingdon Press, 1963.

Pfeiffer, C. F., and Harrison, E. F. *The Wycliffe Bible Commentary*. Chicago: Moody Press, 1962.

Schultz, Samuel J. *The Old Testament Speaks*. New York: Harper & Row, 1960.

Skinner, John. *Isaiah*. 2 vols. Cambridge: University Press, 1951.

Smith, George Adam. *The Book of Isaiah*. London: Hodder & Stoughton. 1900.

Wright, G. Ernest. *Isaiah*. Layman's Bible Commentaries. Richmond: John Knox Press, 1964.

Young, Edward J. *New International Commentary on the Old Testament*. Grand Rapids: William B. Eerdmans Publishing Company, 1964.

---

* The listing of these books does not imply endorsement of their total contents by author or publishers of *The Gospel in Isaiah*.

For Review and Written Work

CHAPTER 1

1. List some of the evidences of the enduring influence of the prophecy of Isaiah.

2. List some marks of greatness which the prophet Isaiah possessed.

3. In what chapter are the call and response of Isaiah related?

4. List the kings of Judah during Isaiah's ministry.

CHAPTER 2

5. List the main themes that constitute the message of the book of Isaiah.

6. For what reasons does Isaiah say Israel's sins were an offense before God?

7. Why was God displeased concerning Israel's religious ceremonials or fasts?

CHAPTER 3

8. The greatest emphasis in Isaiah 40 is _____.

9. The climactic note of the "voices" which speak in Isaiah 40:1–11 is _____.

10. The deliverance of Judah, foreseen in Isaiah 40, was to be from what and under what ruler?

CHAPTER 4

11. List the special verbs and phrases used in Isaiah 41:10–14 to express assurance to God's people.

12. According to Isaiah 42:10–12, how far-reaching is to be the mission of God's Servant?

13. List three reasons given in Isaiah 43:1 for removal of fear.

CHAPTER 5

14. List some of the reasons set forth in Isaiah 43:11–13 and 44:6–8 for knowing the greatness of God.

15. What human folly is discussed in Isaiah 44:9–20?

16. What evidence is given in 45:9–12 of the futility of striving with God?

CHAPTER 6

17. List at least five things foretold about Jesus in the prophecy of Isaiah.

18. What does the name "Immanuel" mean?

19. What titles, according to Isaiah 9:1–7, were to be given to the Suffering Servant?

CHAPTER 7

20. What three great facts are set forth in Isaiah 52:13–15?

21. What was the predicted response of men to the suffering of the One depicted in Isaiah 53:3?

22. For whom was the Servant in Isaiah 53 suffering? for himself, or others?

23. What was to be the effect (or value) of the suffering portrayed in Isaiah 53?

24. How much of the world was to be affected by the salvation promised in 52:10 and 53:1–4?

25. How lasting was to be God's covenant with his people?

26. What new element is added in Isaiah 55:6–7 to the invitation to salvation expressed in the prophecy?

CHAPTER 9

27. What are the three R's upon which true religion rests according to Isaiah?

28. Which in God's sight is more important: religious rites such as fasting, or justice and compassion?

29. For sinful people to be rightly restored to God, what is basically necessary (Isa. 57:15)?

CHAPTER 10

30. Name several of the blessings assured in the new heaven and new earth promised in 65:17-25.

31. What is the chief proclamation of 66:18–25?

32. Amidst the glories revealed for the future of those who trust God, what solemn note is also sounded?

Helps for the Teacher

Prepared by Mavis Allen

Preparation

Skim all of Isaiah, then read with greater care the selected portions for this study. Chapter titles and the passages on which each chapter is based are given in the outlines below:

CHAPTER 1

Backdrop to a Remarkable Prophecy

I. THE TOWERING INFLUENCE OF THE BOOK
1. Its Influence on Hebrew History
2. Its Influence on the New Testament
3. Its Influence on Evangelism and World Missions

II. THE PROPHET ISAIAH
1. The Limited Data About Him
2. The Vastness of the Man
3. His Call and Commitment

III. THE WORLD IN WHICH ISAIAH SERVED
1. His Own Nation
2. The International Scene as Related to Judah

CHAPTER 2

The Message of the Book

I. THE OFFENSE OF MAN'S SINS (1:2-4; 29:13-17)
1. God's Complaint Justifiable (1:2-4)
2. The Nation's Guilt Inexcusable (29:13-17)

II. THE WARNINGS AND PLEAS OF GOD PROCLAIMED (1:10-20, 24-31; 65:1-3)
1. Condemnation of Vain, Meaningless Religious Rites (Activities) (1:10-18)
2. The Cost of Offenses Against God (1:20-31)

III. THE HOPE OF REDEMPTION ASSURED TO A REPENTANT REMNANT (1:9,19; 10:19-22; 46:3-4; 65:8-10)

IV. THE EMPHASIS OF THIS STUDY

CHAPTER 3

God's Message of Comfort and Assurance

I. HEAVENLY VOICES (40:1–11)
   1. The Comforting Voice (40:1–2)
   2. The Commanding Voice (40:3–6a)
   3. The Concerned Voice (40:6b–8)
   4. The Exultant Voice (40:9–11)

II. THE INFINITE POWER AND WISDOM OF GOD (40:12–17)

III. THE LIVING GOD, NOT HELPLESS IDOLS, MAN'S HOPE (40:18–26)

IV. THE ENDURING AND EMPOWERING GRACE OF GOD (40:27–31)

CHAPTER 4

God's Marvelous Grace

I. GOD'S PEOPLE NEED HAVE NO FEAR (41:10–20)
   1. The Reason to Be Free of Fear (41:10–19)
   2. The Reassurance Provided (41:20)

II. THE GRACIOUS MISSION OF GOD'S SERVANT (42:1–12)
   1. The Mission Defined and the Method Disclosed (42:1–3)
   2. The Extent of the Mission Stated (42:4,6)
   3. The Power for the Mission Provided (42:5)
   4. The Effect of the Mission Outlined (42:7)
   5. The Whole Earth to Be Affected (42:10–12)

III. GOD'S REDEEMING AND RESTORING LOVE (43:1–4)
   1. Further Reason for Removal of Fear (43:1)
   2. The Trials Which Afford No Unendurable Test (43:2)
   3. The Preciousness of God's People in His Sight (43:3–4)

CHAPTER 5

God's Majesty and Power

I. HIS INCOMPARABLE GREATNESS (43:11–13; 44:6–8)

II. His Superiority over Other Powers (44:9–20; 45:9–12, 22–23)
1. The Folly of Idolatry (44:9–20)
2. The Futility of Striving with God (45:9–12)
3. The Hope of All the Earth (45:22–23)

III. His Promise and Power to Keep (49:8–16)

CHAPTER 6

Foregleams of Christ

I. His Name (7:10–16)

II. His Advent (40:3–5)

III. His Titles (9:1–7)

IV. His Mission (61:1–3)

V. His Relation to Israel (11:1–9; 4:2–6)

VI. His Rejection by His People (6:9–12)

VII. His Victory over Death (25:8; 26:19)

CHAPTER 7

The Suffering Servant

I. His Affliction and Exaltation (52:13–15)
1. His Wisdom and Triumph (52:13)
2. His Supreme Suffering (v. 14)
3. His Exaltation Among the Nations (v. 15)

II. His Humiliation and Rejection (53:1–3)
1. The Source of the Question (53:1)
2. The Strangeness of the Servant's Coming (53:2)
3. The Failure of Men to See His Beauty (53:2b)
4. The Response of Men to Him (53:3)

III. His Vicarious Suffering (53:4–6)

IV. His Condemnation and Death (53:7–9)

V. His Servanthood and Satisfaction (53:10–12)

CHAPTER 8
The Good News of Salvation

CHAPTER 9
God's Three R's

CHAPTER 10
For All the World

For extra help in background and enrichment studies, see two recent Broadman releases, *Judgment and Redemption in*

Isaiah by Page Kelley and *God Reigns!* by J. Leo Green. For your convenience in studying, the chapters of these books are correlated with the study course book in the chart below:

Guffin	Kelley	Green
1	1, 2	1, 2, 3
2	3, 5	4, 8, 10
3	6	11
4	7	12, 13
5	7	12, 13
6	4, 5	7
7	9	14
8	9	14, 15
9	———	14, 15
10	———	13, 16

Promotion

Posters, articles in the church paper, and announcements will serve to call attention to the study of THE GOSPEL IN ISAIAH. However, these alone will not create the interest that is necessary for maximum participation. The best promotion will be those activities which cause the people to feel a genuine desire to learn what is in this marvelous prophecy. Consider the following activities to introduce the study of Isaiah.

1. *Presentation of Handel's* MESSIAH.—This could be used as the choir's Christmas music. Or, portions of the music could be sung for two or more Sunday's preceding the date for Bible study to begin. Any part of the oratorio would be appropriate, especially those selections whose texts are taken from Isaiah: "Comfort Ye"; "Every Valley Shall be Exalted"; "And the Glory of the Lord"; "Behold, a Virgin Shall Conceive"; "O Thou That Tellest Good Tidings to Zion"; "The People That Walked in Darkness"; "For Unto Us a Child Is Born"; "Then Shall the Eyes of the Blind Be Opened"; "He Shall Feed His Flock Like a Shepherd"; "He Was Despised"; "Surely He Hath Borne Our Griefs"; "And with His Stripes We Are Healed"; "All We Like Sheep Have Gone Astray."

When the music is sung, use the program notes, introductory remarks, or closing statements to point out the connection between the text of the music and the text of the Bible study.

If you decide not to use Handel's music for one program, you may find that using one chorus to introduce each session of the study would provide brief and meaningful worship experiences.

2. *A series of sermons.*—A brief series of sermons based on selected texts from Isaiah could be used to stimulate interest in further study. If such a plan is followed, it would be helpful to read the textbook by Guffin and avoid getting into matters which will be covered in the study.

3. *Filmstrip.*—*The Gospel in Isaiah,* a filmstrip prepared for use with this study course book, is available in Baptist Book Stores. One very excellent way to make use of this resource and to stir interest in the coming study would be to show the filmstrip, announce plans for the study, and have study course books, study guides, and enrolment slips available.

4. *Involvement.*—Plan to preregister by Sunday School classes and departments. Make study course books and study guides available in each department one week before study begins. Ask the superintendent of departments to place some books and enrolment slips in each classroom. It would be helpful if this plan were discussed in the officers and teacher's meeting prior to the emphasis Sunday. Teachers may want to make plans to contact absentees and explain the study to them.

Special Study Guide

A 48-page *Study Guide for The Gospel in Isaiah* is available from your Baptist Book Store. This study aid contains the selected study passages and questions to guide in study. The passages are printed from the American Standard Version, with wide margins for notetaking. These workbooks can be used as assignments for class preparation, for makeup work, or for home study credit.

Teaching Tips for Study Sessions

Chapter 1.—This is a pivotal session. An understanding of the prophet and his time is vital to understanding the message of the book. If you have not already shown the filmstrip on Isaiah, this would be a good time to do so. Then ask those who have study guides to fill in answers to questions 1–3 for chapter 1. For those who do not have the workbooks, the questions are as follows: (1) Write what you believe to be the main ideas in the book of Isaiah. (2) List evidences that the Isaiah prophecy strongly influenced New Testament writers. (3) Why is the book of Isaiah appropriate for study in a year of evangelism and word missions?

In advance of the session, ask someone to be prepared to discuss the facts that are known about Isaiah and his nation. Ask someone else to describe the international scene at that time. Then spend a few minutes discussing the four words Guffin uses to describe the prophet.

Chapter 2.—This chapter is devoted to a study of the message of the book of Isaiah. You may want to divide the class into small groups and assign the questions below which are adapted from the study guide. Each group should find answers and be ready to report to the larger group. It will be helpful if each person has a study guide of his own. If this is not possible, write the following questions on small slips of paper for distribution: (1) What three great themes constitute the message of Isaiah? (2) What is God's complaint in verse 2? in verse 3? (3) What are some things God had done for Israel at this point in their history? (4) List the verbs in verse 4 which describe Israel's attitude to God. (5) Read 29: 13-17 and select a word to describe Judah. Phrase a description of the people as God saw them. (6) What is the analogy used in verse 16 to disclose Israel's stupidity? (7) Read Isaiah 1: 10-31 and list Israel's sins regarding worship. (8) What things did God say they must do before he would accept their worship? (9) List on the left side of a sheet of paper what you believe to be the sins in America that make our worship unacceptable. On the right side, list what you believe God would have us do to make our worship acceptable. (10) From 1: 20-31, summarize Judah's offenses against God. (11) Paraphrase the verses in Isaiah 1: 10-31 which hold out God's promise to those who will turn from their wickedness. (12) Describe briefly the differences of opinion concerning the authorship of the book of Isaiah.

(Be sure that class understands that whatever one believes about its authorship, clearly Isaiah 40 to 66 relate to the time of the Exile and Restoration.)

If it is not desirable to use the group method, the questions may serve as guides to discussion. Be sure that the discussion includes some Scripture searching activities.

Chapter 3.—For a brief period of worship, begin session by reading Isaiah 40: 12-17. Ask four persons to serve as "voices" and share the information from Isaiah 40 and from chapter 3 of the textbook, pages 27-31.

Point out that Isaiah 40: 12-17 teaches both the power and wisdom of God. Ask class, as someone reads the passage aloud, to listen for the three questions that are asked about God.

Ask another person to read Isaiah 40:18–31 while the group listens and notes those verses which give the following answers: (1) the ways men tried to substitute for God; (2) phrases which describe the greatness of God; (3) an answer for the theory that "God is dead"; (4) assurance that God understands man's needs. Close this session by asking group to imagine themselves weary exiles far from the City of God while you read again verses 28–31.

Chapter 4.—Begin the session by reading Isaiah 41:10–20, noting the verbs of assurance there. Note the portion that reflects God's mercy to an unworthy Israel. Ask: What was the purpose of God's phenomenal help for Israel? Is there any parallel for our nation at this point?

If class members do not have study guides, distribute paper for writing the answer to the following question: From a study of 42:1–12, write a brief description of the Servant of God, his mission and method. Ask volunteers to share what they have written. Ask: Who do you think was the Servant pictured here?

In a discussion of 43:1–4 ask that class note: the verbs of assurance; (2) the threefold threat; a conquest foretold; and (3) the unusual way God chose to redeem Israel. Read again verses 1–4.

Chapter 5.—This session can be based entirely on questions from the study guide. The class may be divided into groups, work as individuals, or, you may want to lead a discussion on the questions. In the latter case, those who have study guides may fill in answers as the discussion proceeds. Questions are as follows: (1) What claims does the prophet make for God in Isaiah 43:11–13? (2) How would you define idol worship? (3) In this section of Isaiah (44:9–20), the prophet indulged in sharp satire to drive home the folly of idol worship. List the things you think a modern Isaiah would call idols in our land. (4) To what plight of Israel did Isaiah 49:8–16 apply? What in this passage could be called "The Gospel in Isaiah"? (5) How did God answer Zion's accusation that he had forsaken her?

Chapter 6.—Begin this session with a description of the situation in Israel when the message of Isaiah 7:10–16 was spoken. Ask all who have varied translations of 7:14 to read their translation. (Four are found in the study guide and one in the textbook.) Ask someone to point out the word which has been discussed a great deal. Allow class members to express their viewpoints and present your own. Then, be sure that class understands that the real point of this verse, regardless of translation of *almah*, is the name of the child. Ask class to give name and its meaning—Immanuel, God with us.

The important part of this chapter may be discussed by several persons by assignment or by a discussion which you lead to discover what the prophet gave in the way of foregleams of the Christ: his advent, 40:3–5; his titles, 9:1–7; his mission, 61:1–3; his relation to Israel, 11:1–9 and 4:2–6; and his rejection by his people, 6:9–12; and his victory over death, 25:8 and 26:19.

Allow time for class to give consideration to the following questions taken from the workbook: Read Isaiah 61:1–3 and list some groups who would be among those to whom Christ would minister today. List also some ministries which you feel Christ would perform for such groups.

Chapter 7.—If you have access to a recording of *Messiah*, begin the session by playing choruses based on passages discussed in this chapter: "He Was Despised"; "Surely He Hath Borne Our Griefs"; "And With His Stripes We Are Healed"; "All We Like Sheep."

Ask class to examine 52:13–15 to find phrases which found ultimate fulfilment in Christ. Explain the meaning of phrases or words: "my servant shall deal prudently"; "many were astonished at thee"; "sprinkle"; "sorrows"; "griefs."

Ask group to read 53:1–3 and suggest who the speaker is. What description would sound strange to a farmer?

Lead class to examine 53:4–6 to find evidence of God's mercy and kindness to sinful man. Ask them to look for words or phrases which indicate that the suffering was vicarious, voluntary, and mediatorial. Ask someone to read Matthew 8:17; 1 Peter 2:25; John 10:11; and 1 Peter 2:24 to find ways that Jesus fulfilled this prophecy.

Ask someone to go to the chalkboard and list, as class recalls, the steps in Jesus' trial and death which could be described by phrases from Isaiah 53:7–9.

Chapter 8.—Note that through the years men have told themselves that you don't get something for nothing. Ask if this were true of Israel's release from captivity, our release from sin. Discuss the paradox of a free yet costly redemption.

Ask a good reader to read Isaiah 52:1–3 and 55:1–2 while

the class listens for a description of the hope offered Israel and the parallel hope for all mankind.

To point up Israel's responsibility for her release from captivity, lead in an examination of 52 : 10; 55 : 4.

Ask the entire class to read Isaiah 55 : 1–3a and write a paraphrase with which someone today could be told of Christ's invitation. (Those who have study guides will find space for this activity there.)

As class follows, read 55 : 6–9 and note a new element added to the invitation in 55 : 1 and the condition to be met by those who seek forgiveness. Read 55 : 10–13 and relate this promise to evangelism and world missions.

Chapter 9.—In advance, ask three competent Sunday School teachers to assist in this session by preparing talks on the three R's Dr. Guffin discusses in this chapter.

If there is time, lead the class to fill in blanks for chapter 9 in the study guide. Major questions are as follows: (1) List Israel's unrighteousness as it is noted in this passage. (2) From 58 : 6-7, how would you describe God's righteousness? (3) List the rewards of righteousness as shown in 58 : 8–12.

Chapter 10.—If you did not use the filmstrip *The Gospel in Isaiah* to begin this study, it could be used profitably as a review at this point.

Close the study on a high note of inspiration with a sermon based on the following points:

1. A Glorious Ingathering (56 : 6–8; 60 : 3–7)
2. A New Heaven and a New Earth (65 : 17–25)
3. All Nations to See His Glory (66 : 18–24)

A season of prayer for the Crusade of the Americas and for your church's part in it would be an appropriate conclusion to this session.